a
TREEHOUSE
of your own

The tree before work commenced on our treehouse construction.

a TREEHOUSE
of your own

JOHN HARRIS

BARRON'S

A note on metric equivalency

Throughout the main text of this book, we have included metric equivalents for all measurements. However, to convert the measurements contained in the green "materials boxes" throughout, please consult the chart on page 143.

First edition for the United States, its territories and dependencies and Canada first published in 2005 by Barron's Educational Series, Inc.

Produced by PRC Publishing
The Chrysalis Building
Bramley Road, London W10 6SP
An imprint of **Chrysalis** Books Group plc

All inquiries should be addressed to:
Barron's Educational Series, Inc.
250 Wireless Boulevard
Hauppauge, NY 11788
www.barronseduc.com

International Standard Book No. 0 7641-2906-6

Library of Congress Catalog Card No. 2004109460

Printed in Malaysia

9 8 7 6 5 4 3 2 1

Contents

Introduction

Maybe you were lucky enough to have a treehouse as a child…

A child's treehouse with a large play deck suspended between pine trees.

Or you may have always wanted one, but never had a suitable tree. Possibly you have decided that now is the time to make a peaceful retreat for yourself—somewhere to entertain friends and family. As parents, you may feel that it would be good for the children to have a place of their own, outside, away from computer games in a world of make-believe and adventure.

You may feel that the idea of going to work each morning in a treehouse in your own backyard would aid your creativity, in which case a "tree office" may be the ideal solution. Or it may be that the idea

This young child is showing his love of climbing trees at a very early age.

extremely simple. The floor was an old pallet placed between the three spreading branches of an old apple tree close to the side door of my childhood home. There were walls on only two sides, consisting of discarded doors; there was no roof or windows; no furniture or creature comforts, but it was my special place. Every time I climbed the rickety ladder it was a great adventure. My treehouse was my place—it became a castle, a galleon or a spaceship, and I became Robin Hood, a pirate, or a superhero. I clearly remember attaching a wicker basket to a rope and patiently persuading my small kitten to stay in the basket while he was hoisted up to visit my treetop retreat.

It was these memories of my own childhood that convinced me that I should construct a treehouse

of a secret place equipped with a comfy chair, TV, fridge, and rope ladder appeals to you as the perfect place to watch the big game in peace. Whatever your ideas and motivations, planning and building your own treehouse is a wonderful experience.

It is quite likely that you have not climbed many trees since you were a small child; unfortunately, we all stop doing some of the most simple yet most exhilarating things as we grow up and become more "sensible." Luckily, planning and constructing a treehouse allows you to regain the excitement of carefully pulling yourself up and climbing—sometimes precariously—along branches.

Hopefully you will go on to achieve the satisfaction of completing an aerial dwelling, high above the ground, and the peace and tranquility that only sitting among the leaves in a living tree can create.

I was one of the lucky ones—my father built me a treehouse when I was a very small boy. It was

The author's first self-built treehouse, constructed for his two sons Ross and Fraser.

for my own two boys, who were at that time, four and six years of age. Already I could see the hypnotic effect of the television and the early versions of computer games becoming the focus of their world. I was concerned that unless they had the right "equipment," their ability to create their own games and entertainment would be stifled. And I was worried, too, about the restricted time they spent outdoors.

My first treehouse project was a fairly simple affair, perched on the top of a broken bough of an elm tree close to our house. Clad with cedar shingles on both the walls and the roof, it had a small door,

A treehouse high in an oak tree built in sloping woodland, with a rope ladder and a rope bridge to a tree deck in the distant tree. The flag is flying to indicate that the children are on board.

The author in front of a recently completed treehouse.

formed, and, quite obviously to me, a new world of imagination started to open up. A bent twig became a gun, a handkerchief was transformed into a parachute and our dog suffered the indignity of being lifted into their new castle in the sky.

The magic of their treehouse continued for many years, and I hope it will last in their memories forever. This experience gave me the idea that other people may have the same dreams for their children but may not have the carpentry abilities or time to allow these dreams to be fulfilled. Over several years, this thought developed until I finally decided to do something about it.

I am now uniquely privileged; I design and build treehouses for a living. I travel the world meeting the most interesting people, and advise them on the art of treehouse construction. My Monday morning often starts with me standing high in the boughs of a giant tree surveying not only the tree itself but also the surrounding landscape. Most weeks I visit treehouses at various stages of production and get enormous satisfaction in watching the progress of a treehouse develop in and around the tree. Often I have the opportunity to go back and visit a client and see the treehouse being used by children and adults alike. To see a tree being appreciated and the owners getting so much from the experience is a great reward indeed.

Even when I am office based, I am surrounded by drawings and photographs of trees and treehouses and my time is split between checking on treehouse plans being prepared by designers and communicating with clients at home and abroad from the very first tentative inquiry through to the final specification of their treehouse.

Quite often the initial inquiry is rather wary, "I hope that you don't think I'm silly, but I've always wanted a treehouse..." is how a lot of the conversations start. I enjoy reassuring them that I certainly

three windows for light, and benches at each side inside. Outside a veranda had a fixed ladder for quick escapes and a rope ladder that could be left hanging loose or fixed to brackets in the ground (mastering a swinging rope ladder takes some time). The finished treehouse fit nicely into the yard and created a feature which drew admiring comments from family and neighbors. More importantly, on the day of the grand opening, when the children were allowed up into the treehouse for the first time, it definitely created the desired effect.

Immediately, it changed the way that the boys played (as well as most of the children of the same age in the town) and the treehouse became their focal point. Games were played, gangs formed, dares per-

This high treehouse is over 20 feet (7m) above the ground and is built in a giant oak with a spiral staircase for access.

creating shadows and shapes normally lost in the canopy. I hope, like me, you find the experience uplifting yet relaxing, and that you continue to enjoy the rewards of your labor for a long time after the memories of the physical exertion involved in building it have left you.

Wondering who would read this book before I started writing it, I imagined that it would cover a wide spectrum of individuals, each with different desires, motivations, abilities and circumstances.

That thought certainly raised a challenge. How could I write a book about building a treehouse that could be followed by everyone; all with different skill sets, varying amounts of available time and money, each with their own dream and every tree being a unique challenge.

The answer is obviously impossible. The treehouse design, planning and construction we have decided to follow in this book, which I consider a medium-sized treehouse, will be beyond the carpentry ability of some readers, yet fairly easy for others. The project is likely to take two people about three weeks of hard work, or many weekends taken over a whole summer—too much time for some people to be able to consider, yet a great project for others. And let's not kid ourselves that this is a budget build. If prospective

The view over the roped railings from the front veranda of a treehouse which overlooks the swimming pool to hills beyond.

don't think they are silly. After all, they're thinking along exactly the same lines as I did. Going back to nature and experiencing the calm that a treehouse instills—sharing a high abode with the squirrels and birds, and taking time to escape from the frantic pace at which many of us live our lives, should be encouraged.

I sincerely hope that once you have decided to build your treehouse, with the help of this book, you achieve the look and end result that you wished for. However, more than this, I hope that when you have completed the difficult and sometimes frustrating task of constructing a treehouse, that you can take the time to enjoy the environment of living (possibly only short term) in a tree. There is a unique sense of being close to nature; the air is clearer and it will likely feel slightly cooler and fresher. Noises are sharper, you will hear the faint rustle in the leaves as a light breeze catches them that you would have missed on the ground. The light is different, dappled and reflected between the branches and leaves; it is broken up, treehouse constructors can get hold of cheap or reclaimed lumber of a similar quality, that will be a huge bonus, but the costs will still add up. If all purchased new, the materials alone make this treehouse quite an expensive proposition, and if added to new specialist tools and equipment, the result is a substantial outlay; easy to justify for some, but not for all.

Finally, I have had the good fortune to have been involved in the design and construction of over 500 treehouses now and I have never come across two trees that were exactly the same. So the chances of a prospective reader having a tree in the right place exactly the same as the one featured, or even similar, will be remote.

So this book does not have to be followed to the letter—it can be followed loosely or dipped in and out of. My ambition when writing it has been to give you an outline of the sequence of events that should be followed in all treehouse projects, and while following the case history of one specific treehouse, give many different examples of others and methods of solving your own problems that will inevitably be faced during the process.

It is vital that you set your sights on a realistic goal, taking into account your own ability and that of anyone you can find to help you. You have to budget your time, your money, and most importantly, make sure that your host tree is able to live up to your plans safely and without causing it harm.

If when first skimming through this book you feel that you should start on a smaller or simpler treehouse, or conversely, if you feel you can take on a much larger and more sophisticated project, I hope this book will serve to give inspiration, and provide ideas and solutions that enable you to create the treehouse of your dreams.

This treehouse has a rope bridge that runs towards the double doors under a sheltered roof overhang.

Variations

Another treehouse on stilts gives a rather oriental look above the pond full of koi carp.

This treehouse is suspended on stilts rather than being supported by trees.

The author's own tree deck with a spiral staircase.

Here we have two treehouses in the same group of pine trees joined together by rope bridges and tree decks.

A simple square treehouse with a fixed ladder and rope detailing.

This treehouse, a difficult one to build, is suspended between three poplar trees, on a small island between two streams.

A treehouse hidden at the edge of the yard, where the lawn meets the trees. It has a fixed ladder to an extended veranda.

A more complex octagonal treehouse with a separate tree deck.

Right: A large, round treehouse within the boughs of a giant oak tree in winter.

Equipment

In an ideal world, when planning your treehouse project, you would create a shopping list of all the pieces of equipment and tools that you require and purchase them in a new, or nearly new, condition. Unless you are intending to create many treehouses in the future, I would certainly advise against blowing the budget on tools. The reality is that you are likely to have some tools already or be able to borrow others, and I would suggest that it may be more sensible to hire specialist pieces of equipment, such as pulleys and blocks, unless you see a long term use for them.

Much of the fun you'll have in tackling your treehouse construction will be solving the problems that will inevitably crop up along the way—methods of building without exactly the right pieces of equipment will, I am sure, be one of those. However, while some of the tools I am about to suggest aren't a prerequisite, others are essential, or at the very least, extremely desirable.

Listed below is the equipment that is best to have at your disposal when you start to build. I have indicated in the guide whether I believe these to be *indispensable* or just plain *useful*.

If I were to choose one single item to strongly recommend you invest in, it would be the best quality battery-operated screw gun that you can afford.

A cordless screw gun/driver can save you many hours of labor and allow you to fix many pieces of wood by yourself that may well have taken two people equipped with just a manual screwdriver. You can also utilize a power drill on a low speed setting, but the electric cable is likely to get in your way, or frustratingly, not be long enough.

My own TreeHouse Company builders, who spend all their time in the field and up in trees constructing treehouses, recommend that you get yourself an 18-volt battery screw gun with at least one spare battery. Personally, I would go for a 14- or 15-volt machine which will be slightly lighter, and while it may not hold its power quite as long (at that stage you just change the battery, which should always be on charge), it is easier to use.

Don't bother with a 24-volt battery gun—they are too heavy and have no significant benefits. Remember to always let the battery fully run down before you change it—otherwise, the battery life will diminish very quickly.

A good quality battery screw gun will be invaluable during this project.

Safety helmet
& safety goggles

If you are planning to work on a treehouse site with many other people at the same time, each completing different parts of the project, safety helmets are mandatory. Also, since it is likely that you will be working by yourself or with a friend, it should always be possible to take care of items falling from above. If in doubt, though, wear a helmet. I would certainly list the use of safety goggles as a vital part of your working procedure. Always wear goggles when using an angle grinder, nail gun, or large bench or table saw; your eyesight cannot be replaced and it is worth the minor irritation of the goggles to protect any risk to them.

Safety gloves & safety boots

You should wear steel-capped safety boots whenever you are working on the treehouse site. While it is not always possible to wear safety gloves, as they can be bulky for detailed jobs, these should be worn wherever possible and always when using an angle grinder, nail gun, router, or any power saw.

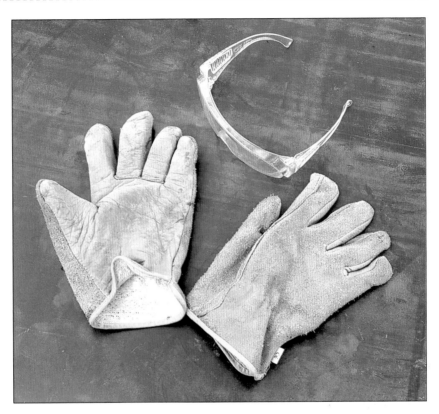

Safety goggles and safety gloves.

Well-worn safety boots.

Safety rope.

Your first aid box can be placed in your home or car when the treehouse project is completed.

A good dry working tent allows you to continue work no matter what the weather, and protects your tools and equipment from the elements.

Ear plugs

It makes practical sense to protect your hearing, but the noise levels created in the construction of your treehouse will be below the level of an average building site. High noise levels are most likely to be confined to the use of power saws and drills. However, please use noise protection if you have sensitive hearing or feel that it is important to you.

Climbing harness & ropes

I cannot believe that it will be possible for you to be able to construct any treehouse where at all times you are safely holding a ladder or standing on a solid and level platform. Therefore you will need to be tied on at some stage. Please do not think that a rope loosely tied around your waist will help you if you fall; it could, in fact, make the situation worse by turning you the wrong way around to land on your head. A simple harness can be worn all the time while building, and clipped on and off as required. Not only will you be safer, you will feel more secure and be able to do the job in hand easier.

First aid kit

Still on safety issues, a well-stocked first aid kit, located close to the build, is another essential. Buying a spare one will stop you dragging muddy boots into the house after a nick or a scrape and it can be relocated for use in the car afterwards.

Storage tent

It may be that you already have some dry storage near the location of the tree. If not, a simple framed tent will do the job. It gives you a base to put things and keeps expensive tools dry during a shower. If you run a power cable to the tent, it will allow you to charge your spare batteries under cover nearby where you are working.

Table saw

Most jobs that will be carried out on a table or bench saw will be possible with a hand or circular power saw, but certainly if you have a table saw available, it will save time and create straighter and more accurate cuts.

Miter saw

The same goes for a miter saw; if you have one, and have the space to install it near the build, then it is a useful addition.

This quality miter saw is built into a work bench.

Power drill & battery drill

Of course it would be possible to construct your treehouse completely by hand without the use of any power tools, but it would be a slow and laborious process. A good 14–18 volt battery screw gun will soon become an extension to your hand and an invaluable aid to the construction and enjoyment of building your treehouse.

Jigsaw & battery jigsaw

There can be no doubt that a good quality jigsaw is vitally important for all aspects of shaping wood and will be required to create the finishing touches and interesting shapes to the exterior of the treehouse. These curves and convolutions cannot be achieved with a straight saw cut. A battery version will make life considerably easier up in the tree, by not having to trail a cable after you, but with careful use of a long extension cord, you can use a conventional power jigsaw. Stock up on replacement blades.

A battery jigsaw.

An angle grinder.

A circular saw.

A nail gun is fairly expensive, but it will save a great deal of time.

Angle grinder **or hacksaw**

The metal brackets and bolts we will be using during the construction will need at worst to be cut and adjusted or at best cut to length to avoid sharp dangerous protrusions. A hacksaw will do the job, but a grinder will tackle these metalwork problems a lot quicker and with a professional finish. Please note an angle grinder needs great care when using; if you have not used one before, make sure someone experienced shows you how to hold it and use it safely.

Circular saw & battery circular saw

A circular saw will certainly speed up the process when trimming decking and, for some jobs, it can be used in place of the table saw, but all its functions could be done with a good, sharp traditional handsaw. As with the jigsaw, a battery version will make life considerably easier.

Nail gun

A nail gun normally powered by a battery or gas is a great tool for speeding up the fixing of interior and exterior cladding, end plates, and finishings. For the average handyman it's a luxury, but as with most luxuries, it's very nice if you can afford it.

Compressor & stapler

Instead of the gas-powered nail gun, you can try using a compressed air machine with nail and staple attachments. It will be fast, (although you will have to make sure you have long enough hoses to reach up into the treehouse leaving the compressor on the ground). The staple attachment is especially good for fixing wooden or felt shingles to the roof.

Hand-held electric router

In many respects I could have easily listed a router (the device that allows wood to be shaped and grooved) as indispensable. Certainly the variation in shapes and textures that it allows on handrails, windows, and internal trims makes it an extremely useful tool that adds greatly to the overall look and professionalism of the finished job. But it's not a must-have, and a good sanding to take the edge off will certainly suffice.

An electric router.

Tool pouch/belt

When you are climbing around a tree and working at height, the less you have in your hands the better, so a tool belt or pouch is a necessity. It will certainly save you many additional climbs up and down for the tool that you didn't think you would need.

A tool pouch / belt.

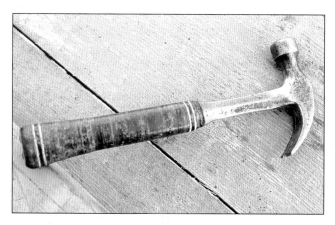

A traditional style hammer.

A budget handsaw can be discarded when blunt.

Hammer

A traditional, well-balanced claw hammer is a versatile and essential tool that should always be on your belt. A lot of craftsmen still swear by a wooden shaft. I prefer fiberglass, preferably in bright yellow so that it is easily visible if dropped accidently into the undergrowth below.

Handsaw

Normally, I would advise that the more you spend on a tool, the longer it is likely to last and perform. In the case of a saw, I don't think this is so. A handsaw needs to be sharp, and unless you are going to spend many hours carefully sharpening a saw blade every few days, I would buy several cheap saws and dispose of them when they are blunt. From experience you will be able to purchase up to six or seven cheap handsaws for the price of one good one; for me, that's certainly better value and more sensible.

Tape measures

You will need a good retractable steel tape measure. A fixed metal rule of about 3 feet (1m) is also useful, as is a plastic soft tape of 40 feet (12m) or so.

A retractable steel tape and folding rule.

Clamps & sawhorses

A selection of clamps and sawhorses will make the work site easier to manage and reduce the need for helpers to hold pieces of wood for you. I would avoid all plastic sawhorses sold in the stores and instead make up some simple A frame sawhorses. Build them at a good working height for yourself using off cuts of lumber left over from the initial construction works.

Knife

I'd be surprised if you did not already have a favorite knife and I know that almost everyone has different ideas about what is good about a certain type or style. I'm sure whatever you have is fine, as long as it is strong and sharp for this job.

Combination square & carpenter's pencil

You are going to need to mark some angles, and a normal pencil is just not up to the job. Purchase three or four carpenter's pencils, as you will surely lose a couple!

A bench made from off cuts.

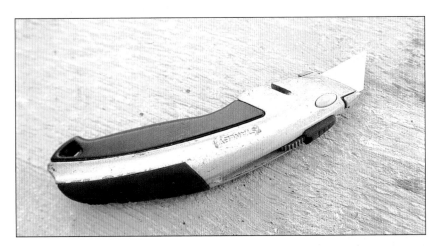
A good retractable knife.

A square and carpenter's pencil.

A set of chisels.

A small socket set should be all you need.

Two spirit levels of different lengths.

Chisels and block plane

A bit like the router I could easily have said that a set of chisels was vital, but you can certainly build a treehouse without. If you are keen to get the finishing, especially the interior just right, I would consider buying a set. (Very few people will lend you chisels, they are quite personal and the sharp edge is easily damaged.)

Socket set

Essential for tightening the large lag screws and bolts for fixing, a good long ratchet handle will save a lot of hard work.

Spirit level

A long spirit level 36″ (91cm) minimum, with 60″ (1.52m) preferred, is an absolute requirement. Please do not be kidded that you can set a long, say 20′ (6m) lumber, off level with a 6″ (15cm) level.

Water level

A water level is not complicated but extremely useful in the environment of a tree with branches that always tend to be in the wrong place. Basically, any long see-through tube with a simple valve or shut off at each end will act as a water level. Fill the tube full with water and seal each end. Put one end slightly higher than the level that you want to follow and the other end again slightly higher than where you think a level should be. Gently open the valves. The water, always finding its own level will slowly settle to exactly level, making it easy to mark.

Extension cord & generator

It's unlikely that you are going to build your treehouse with no power tools, and although you could charge batteries at a distance an extension cable to the site is invaluable. Please remember, if it is a very long distance the power available will drop. It may be that the distance is indeed too far, in which case a generator is required; however, try to avoid this if at all possible as the noise will certainly spoil to some degree the construction process.

Pulley & rope

As you will see when we move on to erecting the platform, a block and tackle or standard simple pulley and rope will be essential to allow the first large wood pieces to be hauled into place.

Ladders

Two sets of extending ladders would be preferable, but you could probably get away with only one. However, then you will be constantly moving and re-tying. Don't even bring stepladders to the site—they are dangerous and unsuitable for outdoor work on uneven ground. If you don't bring them, you will not be tempted to use them!

An electrical generator.

It's important to have a good strong set of extending ladders.

Materials

Here are the four priorities you should have in building your treehouse:

Safety

Tree health

Practicality

Aesthetics

In some cases, the aesthetics (or overall look) can come before the practical usage of the treehouse, but the treehouse users' safety and the health of the tree should always come first.

The materials that we use in the construction of the treehouse very much affect our ability to keep to our priority list above.

1. The main joist and foundation supports must be strong enough to support the load above. The fixings to the tree, or posts to the ground, must be equal to this task.

2. The materials we select which are invasive to (fix into) the tree must not be detrimental to the tree's health and the materials we select to seal around the trunk or branches must be flexible enough not to strangle the tree.

3. From a practical standpoint, the less weight we put up in the tree, the less stress we will put on the tree, and the easier it will be to build.

4. The finished appearance of the treehouse is always a personal issue, but the choice of materials used in the cladding and roofing, as well as the woodstaining color, will obviously have a great impact on the overall effect.

Wood

You may well have a stock or supply of certain types of lumber or you may wish to use some reclaimed lumber that you have available; which is fine, as long as it is fit for the purpose. For the sake of this project, I will assume that you are going to purchase new lumber from a local lumber yard. You can then make your own choices as to what you substitute, according to availability or price, or even the look of the wood. Usually, the wood that we use is softwood. Our preference is for better quality, closer-grained red pine rather than the very soft, yellow variety. This wood should be ordered "pressure treated."

Basically, this method of preserving lumber soaks the dry lumber with the preferred preservative in a sealed tank that is then brought up to a high pressure, forcing the preservative well into the structure of the wood, rather than just coating the outer surface.

The reason we use a soft wood in our construction, rather than as may be perceived "better" hard wood, is weight; we want to reduce the load in the tree as much as possible. For ease of use, softwood is much easier to machine and fix than hardwood and,

Pressure-treated 2 x 3 inch (5 x 7.5cm) structural grade wood.

Round posts used for railings and the staircase.

since we are suspending this structure high off the ground, water will always drain off the treehouse, and therefore the risk of rot in the wood is greatly reduced, making hardwood unnecessary.

The roofing materials used in this treehouse are Canadian cedar shingles. Shingles are thin slivers of wood sawn (although hardwood shingles tend to be split rather than sawn) to a thickness of about ³⁄₈″ (9.5mm) at one end down to very little at the other, with a consistent length of approximately 16″ (40cm), but with a random width. These shingles are laid overlapping as tiles, creating a long-lasting, water-proof, good-looking roof. The beauty of cedar shingles for treehouse construction is that they are very light in weight, flexible to cope with movement and for bending around curved surfaces (as we will be doing in this particular treehouse project), and because cedar has a natural oil, they are long-lasting, without the need for re-treatment.

The other joy of using cedar as a roofing material in a treehouse design is that it will change color depending on the weather and over a period of time. This natural color change—dark brown in the wet and light in the dry, and changing from brown to silver over time—fits well into the natural surround-ings of a tree, which also changes color during the course of the year.

A note on metric equivalency

Throughout the main text of this book, we have included metric equivalents for all measurements. However, to convert the measurements contained in the green "materials boxes" throughout, please consult the chart on page 143.

Everything you will need for this project:

12—2″ x 10″ pressure treated structural softwood (16′ in length)

32—2″ x 8″ pressure treated structural softwood (16′ in length)

1—2″ x 6″ pressure treated structural softwood (16′ in length)

26—2″ x 4″ pressure treated structural softwood (16′ in length)

12—1″ x 1″ pressure treated structural softwood (12′ in length)

94—2″ x 3″ pressure treated structural softwood (12′ in length)

24—½″ x 3″ pressure treated structural softwood (16′ in length)

16—½″ x 1″ pressure treated structural softwood (12′ in length)

30—1″ x 6″ tongue and groove, treated flooring (14′ in length)

84—¾″ x 4″ tongue and groove, treated cladding (16′ in length)

44—1″ x 6″ ribbed redwood decking (14′ in length)

16—2″ round section doweling (12′ in length)

13—1″ round section (12′ in length)

3—1″ x 3″ treated moldings (12′ in length)

5—½″ x 1″ treated moldings (16′ in length)

21 sheets—¾″ exterior grade or marine plywood

1 sheet—¼″ low grade plywood

5—5″ round posts (12′ in length)

3—4″ round posts (16′ in length)

1—4″ round posts (12′ in length)

22 bundles—cedar shingles

lead sheeting

polycarbonate or toughened glass double-glazed sealed units

door and window catches and hinges

20—2″ custom angle brackets

20—metal jointing plates

32—angle stair brackets

¾″ natural fiber rope

½″ natural fiber rope

binding twine

stain and preservative

sealant

wicker basket

zip slide equipment

small pulley

Cedar shingles are conventionally ordered and delivered in bundles, as shown above.

Shingles

Cedar shingles are normally sold by the bundle; you will require 22 bundles for this project. (The lumber yard where you order all the main pieces of wood for this project may be able to supply your shingles, but you may have to find a more specialized supplier.)

Metalwork

While it would be nice to only use wood in the construction of your treehouse, we also need some metal elements for strength of jointing. The screws and bolts are fairly standard, the larger lag screws may need ordering in advance but your local hardware store should be able to supply the items in the list without too much trouble:

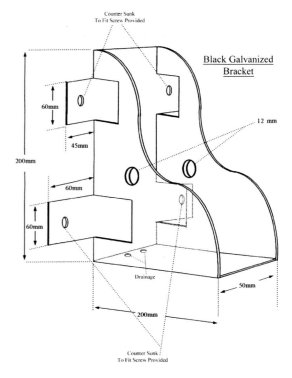

This customized angle bracket will have to be ordered and made in advance to the dimensions and sizes as shown.

You will need to order and organize the main support brackets and jointing brackets well before starting construction. These are very important parts of the foundation construction.

Screws and bolts:

40—½″ x 10″ galvanized lag bolts

20—½″ x 4″ galvanized lag bolts

approx 2000—galvanized brad nails (loose or for a nail gun)

approx 500—½″ galvanized panel pins

stainless steel or zinc-plated wood screws, in the following amounts and gauges:

    250—¾″ x 4

    500—1 ½″ x 6″

    1,000—2″ x 6″

    2,000—2 ½″ x 6″

    250—3" x 8″

    250—3 ½″ x 8″

Flat jointing plates, galvanized before painting (left), and angle brackets, galvanized and painted (right).

The angle brackets shown in the diagram have been developed over time by my company and have proven to be reliable and easy to use. The position of the lag screw holes reduces the risk of damage or decay to the tree and the drain hole at the base allows accumulated dampness to drain off, reducing the risk of rot. The metal tongues can be bent to suit the shape of the tree and, if carefully made by an experienced metalworker or blacksmith, only two welds are needed. The angle bracket and the flat jointing plates should be made from ⅛″ (3mm) steel plate and must be galvanized after fabrication and then painted with recognized metalwork paint. Black or dark brown tends to look best.

Neoprene

To create the waterproof collars that are fitted each time the tree trunk or branches go through the structure of the treehouse, you should use a material called neoprene. The rubber-like sheet material is used in both the car production industry and in the manufacture of wet suits. It has many properties that make it ideal for its purpose in the context of treehouse construction. It is strong yet very flexible, and does not break down or harden over time or when exposed to sunlight. As a rule of thumb, we order 3 square feet (0.27m²) of ³⁄₁₆″ (4.75mm) neoprene for each branch or trunk that will pierce the skin, walls or roof of the treehouse.

Rope

I tend to use rope not only for practical purposes, such as hanging swings or basket pulleys, but also for decoration and filling gaps.

Although a natural rope, such as manila, has the rather annoying characteristic of stretching, it is much more suitable for most purposes in treehouse construction than a manmade rope. It looks better

Redwood ribbed decking.

than brightly-colored synthetic rope, and when wrapped around the tree trunk or branch to hide the internal gap left to allow the tree to grow, it will give and stretch to accommodate the tree rather than potentially strangling it.

Another reason rope is a good filler in the gap around the tree inside the treehouse is that it allows the tree to move in the wind without damage. The rope nicely stops anyone from putting their fingers into the gap with the potentially dangerous result of getting trapped or crushed as the tree moves.

I would advise that you purchase several feet of varying thickness of manila rope for the project.

Polycarbonate

My preferred choice of material for the windows is polycarbonate. It is very strong and flexible, and it allows the treehouse to move and flex in the wind without the risk of cracking.

If, however, the treehouse is situated in the strong base of a large, mature tree where the likelihood of movement is substantially reduced, and if the treehouse is to be insulated, then you can use toughened double-glazed units like the ones we are using for the treehouse in this book. For your first treehouse I would strongly advise polycarbonate of which you will require 50 square feet (4.65m²).

Decking

Use a redwood decking, ribbed on one surface to reduce slipping. Always leave a gap between boards to stop the buildup of water on platforms and the veranda.

Assessing

Our selected oak tree.

One of the greatest challenges in writing this book, which follows the planning, design, and construction of one particular treehouse, is trying to relate the necessary information to the reader while understanding that the tree in which he or she will be building a treehouse is likely to be completely different from the one followed here.

In this case, we have chosen a mature English oak, with a straight and strong trunk, which divides into three main boughs forming an interesting bowl shape, that will eventually be a grand feature inside the treehouse itself.

You may be in the situation where you either have a tree in mind or that there is no other choice other than one particular tree. Conversely you may have many trees to choose from and are hoping that this section of the book will give you the guidance to select the perfect or best tree for your needs.

As a general rule, a treehouse may be built in almost any mature or semi-mature, strong, healthy tree; avoid trees that are too young, show signs of disease or rot, have large gaping holes, or are leaning badly. If it is going to be the sole support of the treehouse, the tree should ideally have a circumference of

This ideal sycamore tree with an obvious, large, low limb will make a great place to build a treehouse.

the good tree husbandry of thinning a tree, I do not condone stripping healthy boughs and branches from a tree in order to create the space for a treehouse. While it is often surprising how much space there is among the branches of a large tree, do not think that you will manage to build your dream treehouse within dense, closely-packed branches. Unless you are lucky enough to have the perfect treehouse tree that opens up like an upturned hand and has lots of space within the bowl, the best approach is to construct around the trunk of the tree before it starts to spread.

Especially for your first treehouse, a platform height of between 10 and 15 feet (3m and 4.5m) is fine, so don't look too high up into the tree; keep your search within the lower parts of the trees.

In cases where the tree is under the ideal circumference, or if the treehouse required is larger than an individual tree could cope with, a treehouse can still be constructed using a group of several trees to distribute the load.

over 5 feet (1.5m) at its base and any main boughs to be used in the design should be over 6 inches (15cm) in diameter at the points where they are to be involved in the construction.

Among the best candidates are oak, beech, maple, lime, ash, chestnut, and mature fruit trees. But you could also consider a multitude of other species from the common fir, larch, spruce, or pine, to the more unusual walnut or hemlock.

Trees like the silver birch and poplar, which have very shallow rooting systems, would not be ideal as the sole support of a treehouse. However, by designing a treehouse on stilts, this type of tree can still be integrated in the treehouse design. For instance, wooden support stilts can be erected to distribute the overall weight and blend naturally into the aesthetics.

Having the space in or around the tree to house the treehouse is also vital. While I agree with

The area within the chosen oak tree in which we will be building the treehouse, before lopping.

In this case, the treehouse is supported on stilts as the tree was not considered strong enough to support the structure itself. It is also close to water which can undermine roots.

One of the main issues to understand is that no matter how good the tree is, if it is in the wrong place, it is not suitable.

As someone who is lucky enough to spend a great deal of my working life wandering around other people's yards and woods, looking for suitable candidates for a treehouse, I fully realize how frustrating this can be. I regularly find a great tree, which is strong and in good condition, the right size and shape, but located in completely the wrong position.

To a certain extent I could argue that the location of the tree for a proposed treehouse is more important than the tree itself. Ultimately, it is a combination of these two factors.

Don't select a tree that is :

1. Nearby to a busy road. A treehouse can be a great distraction for motorists and can cause accidents.

2. Overlooking a neighbor's yard or giving views in though a neighbor's window; respect their privacy as you would expect them to do yours. Sometimes making sure that no windows or verandas look in their direction is sufficient to solve this issue. But always inform your neighbor what you intend to build and if it affects them in any way, BEFORE you start.

3. On a steep slope or directly on the bank of a river. The treehouse foundations are in effect the roots of your host tree; if the tree is on a sharp incline it has had to put its roots out into the hillside to "hold on." Putting additional weight on a tree such as this is not sensible, and if the ground on one side of the tree is being eroded by a river or fast flowing stream, this will also undermine these foundations.

4. Too far away. Although you may well find your ideal tree further away than where you or your children normally roam, don't build a treehouse that will not get used. Unless you specifically require a retreat to be used for occasional visits, the pleasure of a treehouse is being able to use it whenever you feel like it and certainly, in my experience, children will not go outside of their "safe" area.

5. Next to a trail or public footpath. A treehouse is often far too big a temptation for curious passersby, and can attract unwelcome visitors—in some cases, even attacks of vandalism.

The author standing in the chosen tree in the area that will eventually become the table!

The author measuring the exact height of the treehouse platform.

Calculating the heights of the tree's major branches from the ground.

Once you have found your tree and made sure that it is in a suitable location, you can start to focus your thinking on what and where in the tree you are going to build.

It is a great idea, and certainly worth the time, to visit your tree at different times of the day to see where and how the sun strikes it, at the same time trying to visualize how it is at other times of year. Not so difficult in the case of a conifer but vital for all deciduous trees, a treehouse may be quite open in the winter with no leaves on the tree but totally shaded in the summer. More commonly, a treehouse is constructed in the summer months and then creates a shock for neighbors and others when it comes into full view later in the year. So take care.

Before you move on to the exciting stage of planning your treehouse, we need to try and establish two important decisions; platform height and type and direction of access.

You will be measuring the tree carefully during the planning phase. At this stage you are just trying to establish in your own mind at what height the treehouse is best placed, and this will be determined for the most part by the tree. If, in the simplest case, the tree is a straight, tall trunk, rising high into the air before it branches, the platform could be at any height and would be determined more by how you want to access the tree, the ages of adults and children who will use the treehouse, or specific views that you want to try and achieve.

If, as is more likely, the tree has branches within the first 10 to 25 feet (3 to 7.5m), it is these that will probably determine the finished treehouse height. You need to consider whether you wish to build in the branches or under them. It's important that at this stage you make a decision on the preferred height, as it will allow you to get a mental picture.

Remember, exact plans will come later and you can change the decision on platform height at any stage until the plans are finalized.

I always try to position the method of access up into the treehouse from the most frequently used

A treehouse in a mature scots pine within the private boundaries of a formal garden, seen from a distance between two bushes.

direction, that people using the treehouse are likely to follow. You have a choice of a ladder (solid or rope), or a staircase (traditional or spiral). In the case of the treehouse that is being followed in this book, a two-way traditional staircase was decided upon, leading from the grass pathway to the side of the treehouse. It will be very helpful when you come to initial planning that you have a good idea of how you want to climb up to the treehouse and from which direction.

The other aspect of siting the treehouse—one that is often overlooked—is that different views will be opened up from a point that is much higher up in the tree. Now that you have decided what height you think the treehouse platform should be, if you haven't done so already, it makes sense to climb the tree using a ladder and stand at the same height as the completed platform. Then you can assess the views that have opened up before you.

This impressive treehouse has a lower deck around the simple trunk of this large tree and the main treehouse above within the branches as they spread outward.

Planning

You probably want to get started on the "real
work" of building your treehouse, but remember, the time
taken at the planning stage will result in a better end result, and
save you a lot of time and frustration.

I suggest that you go through each of the stages on the following pages to create a full set of plans, and take the time to adapt and improve these until you are completely satisfied.

The first stage is to draw a scale plan (say 1 : 50) of the area surrounding the chosen tree. Mark any features, paths, walls, flowerbeds, buildings, or other trees, the compass direction, and the direction of particularly good views. Show on this plan the

direction in which most people will approach the treehouse and any steep slopes or contours.

This overall site plan will be extremely useful when you come to position the main features of the treehouse, the veranda, balcony, and the main access points; especially if people are to work on the tree in your absence.

The next stage depends very much on the type and shape of tree that you have chosen. If it is a simple, straight up-and-down trunk, with no branches between where you think the platform height will be and for the next 10′ to 12′ (3 to 3.6m) above this, it is not relevant. But if the tree has healthy branches, you need to sketch each side from three or four different points around the tree.

If you title each of these sketches "Elevation 1/2/3," etc. the direction of each can be marked on the site plan. Take some visual points on each of the main branches and measure the height of these to the ground, using the steel tape or a long plastic tape attached to a long, thin stick. Mark these heights on your elevations. As you have already decided where you think the platform height of the treehouse should be, you could mark this on each of the elevation drawings as a solid horizontal line through the tree.

The next stage is one of the trickiest, and will require a degree of imagination. You need to draw a plan of the tree, first at platform height. The best way to approach this is to imagine that a giant knife has

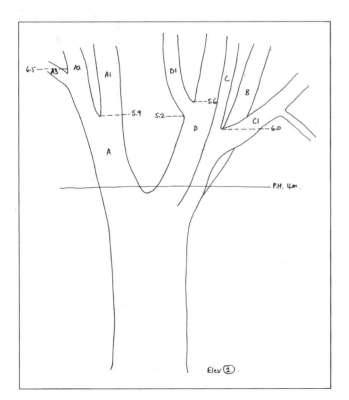

A sketch of our oak tree from the side

cut through the tree at the height of the treehouse platform, and you are looking down on the tree from above.

If the tree at this height is just a simple trunk, you would see only a circle; if the tree had by this height divided into two main trunks, you would see two circles. If you are intending to build within the branches of the tree there could be several lateral boughs and trunks to take into consideration.

At this stage it is necessary to climb up the tree using a ladder and measure the circumference of the trunk and any boughs that are indicated on your bird's eye view plan and also the distances between each of these. This information may then be plotted out to scale (say 1:50).

Once this is complete, it is useful to indicate with an arrow the direction in which any of the main branches rise up and away from the platform height.

With all of this information collated you can now start to design your treehouse. You will see from the elevation of the tree we are using in this book, the platform height is under the height where the trunk

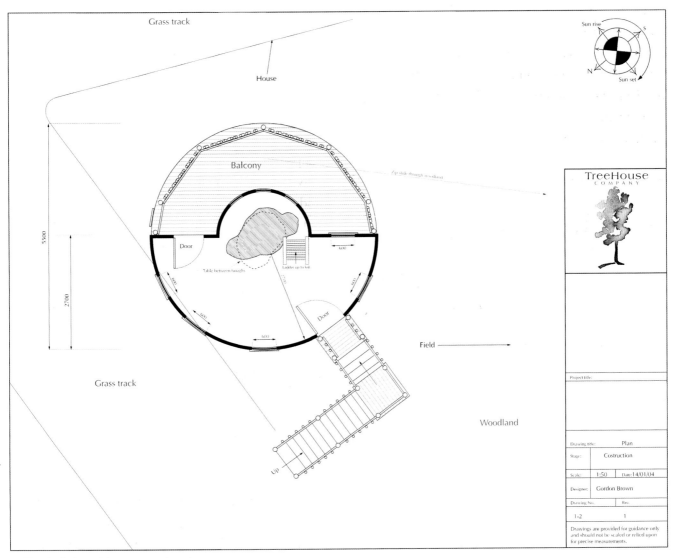

The final plan of the proposed treehouse.

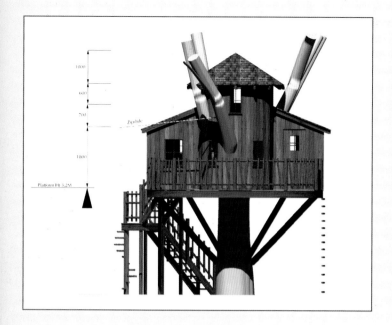

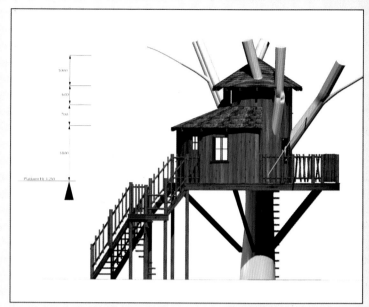

The front view elevation

We wanted a large veranda facing the best views so this was drawn to the southeast, where it will also catch the sunlight from first thing in the morning until late in the afternoon.

The position and type of staircase is an important consideration during this planning stage. I feel that the choice of staircase depends very much upon who will be using the treehouse.

In this case, the treehouse is intended for the whole family, including very young visitors, the family's children, and older relatives; so an easy-to-climb stair was of utmost importance. To make the experience more exciting for the older children, a rope ladder will also be fitted.

Unusually, the clients decided not to have the staircase—being the preferred choice of access to the treehouse—joining the veranda, as it was felt that the treehouse should appear to "float" in the tree when looked at from the front. So the staircase was designed to the rear, with a sheltered doorway leading into the back of the treehouse, which necessitates a second doorway out onto the veranda.

One side elevation

Once the platform area is decided upon, it can be split into inside and outside space and where the stairs or ladders should join. At this stage it is important to keep checking on your drawings, to see where each branch will feature in your design, making sure that they do not run across doorways or access areas. It's likely that you will draw several different variations of the floor plans until you achieve one that will work best with the tree. When you are satisfied with the platform plan you can start to draw the elevations of each wall showing where branches come through, if required. You will see from our elevations that the design ensured that the branches came though the turret wall and roof section of the treehouse (avoiding doors and windows) and gave plenty of head room to walk around the treehouse both inside and out.

Keep taking your plans and drawings back out to the tree to ensure that what you have drawn will work in reality, and you will soon start to visualize the treehouse within the tree, long before the first lumber arrives.

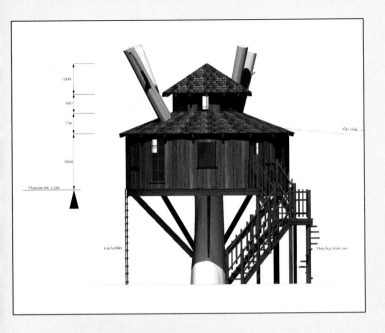

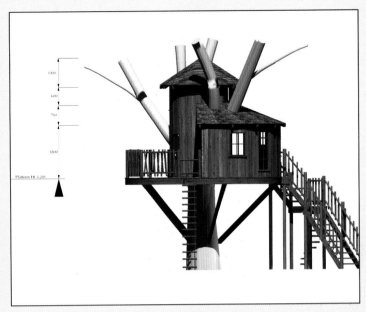

The rear elevation

The shape of the walls and the available space within the tree will determine the roof shape. In this case the idea is to follow the circular shape of the platform with a lower roof level around half of the tower, and then have a true turret roof high into the space created by the spreading tree boughs. It's a good idea to draw a separate roof plan, as this will help greatly when it comes to constructing the roof itself.

Remember, in some areas you may need local government planning consent before you embark on your project, and they will doubtlessly need to see the plans that you have drawn up at this stage.

Calculating the lengths of the wood pieces required for the bracers and treehouse foundations.

The other side of the treehouse

The final requirement in planning your treehouse is finalizing and drawing the supporting wood pieces. Depending on the finished plan size of your treehouse—and the size of the tree—you can work out how many bracers and/or posts that are going to be required to support it. Generally you will require at least one method of support for each corner of the structure, and in the case of our round treehouse, eight 45-degree knee bracers are going to be used. Each of these should be drawn on to your floor plan and each of the elevations. Although the bracers do not need to reach to the outside edge of the platform, make sure that they go at least two-thirds of the way. A 45-degree bracer is the strongest method of transferring the load from above down the trunk of the tree to the ground below. It is better to keep all the bracers to the same angle and vary their length, as this will stop them all meeting the tree trunk at exactly the same height above the ground. This reduces the risk of damage to the tree by boring too many holes around the girth of the tree at the same height.

Planning the foundation wood pieces to this degree of accuracy will allow you to approach the final preparation, before construction, with confidence.

Above: Our computer-generated perspective presentation of the proposed treehouse, created before we started to build. Compare how it looks against the completed treehouse. Right: The finished treehouse just before the oak emerges into full leaf in late April.

splits and therefore only the trunk affected the design at this height.

However the trunk splits into four main boughs approximately 3 feet (1m) above this height, so great care had to be taken to accommodate these large limbs as they run through the treehouse and out through the walls and roof.

In this case, we have decided on a circular shape and as the tree divides and opens, it creates a large void toward the center of the tree above the platform height. We are going to design a turret or tower as a second floor area.

At the TreeHouse Company, we have at our disposal a software package that allows us to design the proposed treehouse in three dimensions and then transpose the design on to a photograph of the tree that is being considered for the build. This enables us to show our clients a very good representation of the completed treehouse before they decide to proceed with the project.

Preparing to Build

By now you will have thought about how you are going to approach
the build phase of your treehouse—whether you are going to
complete it in one period of time, tackling it over several weekends, or
waiting until the summer.

The author taking his client through the plans and elevations drawn up in advance.

However you decide to build your treehouse, you
need to order all the materials well in advance
and make sure everything you require to complete the
project is on-site before you begin. You don't realize
how much time can be lost by hanging around

waiting for something to arrive or having to go away
from site to collect some missing component!

You should create a complete material order
list and split this into different types of materials
(timber, rope, metal work etc) and give it to several

A safety barrier will keep the curious and unwary at bay.

suppliers to price. After comparing prices, quality and availability, place your orders to be delivered to the site at a time when you can be there to check everything off and make sure that they are all of the quality you require. You also need to ensure that you have adequate access for the delivery vehicles and that you know where everything is going to be stored.

The timber which is going to take up the majority of the space will all be treated, so it will not be damaged by being left open to the elements. However cutting dry timber is much easier than wet, so if possible, cover all materials carefully as soon as they arrive with large tarpaulins. Obviously, the closer you can have the materials delivered to the tree the better. The next task is to move everything to its final

Unloading materials as they are delivered to the site at the beginning of the project. Carrying and storing all the materials close to the tree saves a lot of time.

You can protect the ground at the base of the tree with a lightweight canvas. Not only will this make it easy to recover items inadvertently dropped during the build, but it will also keep the high-traffic area around the base firm and dry.

resting place before being lifted into the tree. Make sure you stack all materials in a convenient place so they won't have to be double-handled. Don't be tempted to try to build your treehouse by bringing materials from a distance, as they are needed; it wastes far too much time.

Create a "No Go" area in the immediate vicinity of the tree and ensure that children and casual observers keep out of the area.

It is important that visitors to the site where you are constructing your treehouse are fully aware how close they can come to the tree in safety. The best way I have found is to create a visual line around the treehouse site with colored tape, at about 3 feet (1m) above the ground. When you are working on a

formal lawn, it is also a good idea to cover the area immediately around the tree with tarpaulins to protect the grass and keep the mud at bay during wet weather.

Next you will need to get the safety ropes into place. The way to do this is by throwing, or shooting, a weighted object with a thin line attached over branches higher than the highest point of the treehouse. This line is attached to the climbing/safety rope which is hauled into place by carefully pulling on the thinner line. I have experimented with sling shots, catapults, and even a bow and arrow, and for my money the best and easiest way is to throw a soft, weighted bag made from a piece of cloth filled with wet sand or small pebbles, and tied tightly shut. Don't try to get a head start and climb a ladder to throw the weighted bag, it is not safe and you are unlikely to throw any further than you can with a much better stance from the ground. Start from the ground and throw until you achieve the best height that you can. As long as this is well over platform height this is fine, as you can always raise the height once a solid and safe platform is in place.

I prefer to set two or three different lines in different places at this stage, so I can move comfortably in all parts of the tree just by changing ropes. Once you have pulled the light rope though the branches and this has brought the safety rope back to you, tie a bowline or slip knot and leave your safety lines hanging in place until you need them.

You can also use the same method to attach your pulley hoist high above the working area. When tying your bowline knot, attach the pulley with its own rope to the loop, feed the end of the rope you were going to pull into the tree through the loop, and raise the pulley up into the tree.

It's a good idea at this stage to test your climbing harness and to make sure that you are confident about using it before starting to build. As high as you

The tree after the dead wooding was carried out, with the dead wood ready to be removed from the site.

The author making a final check on the height of the turret section of the proposed treehouse.

can reach comfortably, take a section of the hanging safety rope in your hand, make a loop between your thumb and index finger, loop this around the back of the hanging rope and thread it between the two, pull tight and you will create a permanent loop hanging from the safety rope. You can do this as many times and at as many heights as you require up the entire length of the safety rope. Clip a carabiner with a screwgate through the D ring on the safety harness and on to the loop on the safety rope, sit down on the harness and take the weight off your legs; you will hang quite happily in your harness. Take a few minutes to get used to the feeling and you will realize that you are quite safe and able to work at heights as long as you are clipped on properly.

Now is the stage when you should start preparing and setting up your tools. If possible the bench saw or table saw should be under cover. Level, strong, workbenches and cutting tables should be erected in a convenient location for both the stored lumber and access to the tree.

Unless a generator is going to be used, the electric extension cables should be run to the site and the cable carefully marked and pegged down to stop someone tripping over it. If you are using a generator, ensure that any spare fuel is located safely a long way away from the site. Batteries for any battery operated hand tools should be put on charge and you should make a final check that everything is in place and ready to start building.

Please remember that whoever is going to be helping you in the construction of your treehouse needs to be fully briefed of all aspects of site safety, and has a full and detailed understanding of what is required of him or her. At this stage any dead wooding that needs to be carried out should be done before the treehouse is started. In this case several branches were dead and had to be removed.

Foundation

The aim is to construct a level and strong base for your treehouse, floored partially in smooth floorboards and the rest in ribbed timber decking.

For your completed treehouse to be safe, long lasting, and attractive, each of the processes outlined in the subsequent chapters of this book need to be followed carefully. However, none more so than this section on the treehouse foundation. Completed successfully, the foundation will be level and strong, and provide the perfect platform on which to start the construction of the treehouse walls and roof.

Throughout this book, you will see examples of several methods of platform support and ways of suspending the treehouse platform in or around the tree. Some of these other examples are described at the end of this chapter but all have one thing in common; they are designed to create a base on which the treehouse fabric is erected, while at the same time allowing the tree to continue to grow without restriction.

Time spent ensuring that the platform is absolutely level will be well worthwhile. The majority of the structural strength of the treehouse is created during this stage.

After all the planning and preparation, at last you are ready to build. We will show in this chapter how to place the all-important first pieces of wood, and how to attach them without harming the tree. At this stage, we will install the first horizontal struts, supported by the 45-degree knee bracers that will ultimately take all the weight of the treehouse down the trunk of the tree. On top of these first structural planks will lie the network of joists, onto which we will attach the base platform of internal and external flooring of the first level.

Safety

During the construction of the treehouse foundations, we will be climbing our tree for significant lengths of time and handling the largest and heaviest of the lumber; at all times during this stage safety must be at the forefront of your mind.

SAFETY CHECK

• **Have at least two people present at all times during this stage.**

• **Wear the appropriate safety equipment.**

• **Use a safety harness and ropes at heights.**

• **Securely tie the tops of all ladders while being held by your helper.**

• **Never stand on the foundation or platform until it is tied together to form a solid base.**

Key objectives

- Place the main supporting planks in position as planned.
- Join these to the tree, creating a permanent and strong fixing.
- Establish a level platform.
- Fix together with joists in the correct position to add the flooring materials.
- Complete the foundation to size and shape.
- Attach the internal and external flooring, leaving room for tree growth.
- Make a strong and stable platform from which to start the treehouse walls.

Note: The construction of a treehouse of this size is a two-man job and for safety reasons, only the final stages should be carried out alone. At this stage, if at all possible, you should recruit further help.

The strong, level deck during the flooring stage.

Leveling a treehouse platform before decking.

EQUIPMENT

Essential
power drill
jigsaw
handsaw
tape measure
spirit level
hand tools

Useful
battery drill
water level
pulley and rope

MATERIALS

32—2″ x 8″ pressure treated structural softwood (16′ in length)
30—1″ x 6″ redwood tongue & groove flooring (14′ in length)
38—1½″ x 6″ treated ribbed redwood decking (14′ in length)
20—2″ custom metal galvanized angle bracer brackets
20—galvanized metal jointing plates
hardwood off-cuts for wedges

It will be possible for two people to complete the foundation, but another one or two extra pairs of hands will make a big difference. So if you have any favors to call in, arrange to do so over the days where you are taking on steps 1 and 2 of this stage.

We have already established the height at which the treehouse platform will be constructed and so our first task is to fix the initial bracket that will set off the entire treehouse construction. With bracket, 10″ (25cm) lag screws, tape measure, wrench, and drill, climb the fixed ladder till level with the platform

Measure and mark the height of the platform exactly as planned.

Pre-drilling the tree trunk ready to accept the lag screws.

level mark you have made. Attach the bracket and drill with short lanyards slightly higher on the ladder, and position the first bracket 10″ (25cm) below the platform mark, at the point we have determined the

Fixing the first bracket in place with lag screws.

A correctly fitted bracket showing the wedge in position.

Marking the foundation lumber to length.

Cutting the foundation lumber to length.

You will save time by pre-drilling the support lumber.

first joist will sit. Mark the screw holes onto the trunk and drill pilot holes to a depth of approximately 7″–8″ (18–20cm).

Using the wrench on a ratchet setting, screw the bracket into the tree, making sure it is vertical in towards the tree trunk. At this stage, don't tighten it flush to the trunk.

As the bracket is pulled towards the trunk, you will start to see at what angle the bracket will lie when fully tightened. You will also be able to measure the size of the wedge that will be required to fit behind the bracket, to make sure that when tightened it will sit upright and enable the joist to be perfectly horizontal. You may be lucky, because at this point the tree may be flat and vertical allowing the bracket to

The first horizontal joist is hauled into place using ropes.

Make sure these main wood pieces are precisely horizontal before fixing them into position.

sit exactly right, but it is very unlikely that this will be the case all around the tree at the point of each bracket fixing. Back on the ground, cut the appropriate wedge to the correct size and shape. Remember that time spent at this stage will pay massive dividends later with a completely flat platform. Sliding the wedge behind the bracket, the lag screws can be tightened and the bracket fixed into its final position.

During the planning phase we have established that the main horizontal lumber will protrude from the main tree trunk by approximately 14′ (4.2m). However, as the tree trunk is unlikely to have grown perfectly straight and vertical, and we want to achieve as perfect a circular treehouse as possible, we will fit these at 16′ (4.8m) and shorten them at a later stage.

There are two methods to keep the first horizontal lumber in place while we attach the knee bracers, and in this treehouse we will use a combination of both. First, we can support the lumber at the outside end with a tall vertical pole placed on the ground, either pinned or tied to the main lumber at the correct height. This is ideal for the first joist as it

fixes the height of the platform and does not need to be leveled off with other joists. Measure two thirds of the length of the joist and make a mark on the underside, then attach the free end of a flexible tape measure at this point with a small screw.

Tie both ends of the first 2″ x 8″ (5 x 20cm) joist to the hauling ropes that should be placed through the pulleys attached to the higher branches.

The joist is now carefully raised into the tree— with you already up the ladder—ready to receive the end closest to the trunk. You will need to be equipped with a long spirit level attached to a lanyard. Take care not to damage any branches as the joist is hauled up. Once you get a hold of your end of the joist, carefully slide the end into the bracket and swing the joist out so that it lies on the correct line out from the tree. Once approximately level and in the correct position, use the spirit level by lying it on the top edge of the joist to check, while asking the rope handler to lower or raise the joist until it's perfect.

At this stage the rope can be either tied off or continued to be held, if you have spare help available.

Holding the first foundation lumber carefully in place.

Once the knee bracing wood is married up to the joist, it can be cut to the correct angle and bolted on using the joining plates.

At the point you marked earlier, approximately two thirds of the way along the joist, a tall temporary support can now be gently positioned against the joist. Then, using the tape measure previously attached, measure the height from the ground to the lower side of the joist. Make a note of this measurement. Next, take the tape towards the tree and, keeping exactly in line with the joist above, pull taught to make an angle of approximately 45 degrees to the trunk, note the measurement at this position and make a mark on the tree trunk. Once these measurements are established, the joist can be taken out of the bracket and carefully lowered back to the ground.

Attach a second bracket, in the way you did previously for the joist, in the position marked on the

trunk for the knee bracer, and cut slightly over-length the temporary support and the 2″ x 8″ (5 x 20cm) knee bracer support. Attach the support post to the side of the joist with two screws, so the height you measured is level with the lower side.

The joist can now be raised again, this time permanently, into position. Make sure that the support post is pulled upright into position without catching on ground cover or branches. Once vertical, the support post will sit on the ground and after checking again for level, the joist can be bolted to the brackets using lag bolts.

Very carefully, using ropes and a climbing harness, it is now time to haul up the knee bracer. While fitting into the lower bracket against the tree trunk,

The first few foundation wood pieces are put into place, with the supporting post keeping the new joist horizontal.

mark along the underside of the first joist against the bracer joist to ensure the exact angle for the cut. At the same time, the tape measure may be unfastened. Lowered again to the ground, the bracer can be cut to the correct angle at the top to fit under the joist and at the bottom to fit precisely into the bracket.

Once cut to length, it can be hauled into place and carefully bolted to the top joist using the flat plates, one on each side, again with lag bolts. This process needs to be repeated for each of the joists and bracers as planned (in this case, ten times!).

Each of the joists and 45-degree knee bracers are fitted into place making a cartwheel around the tree trunk. It is vital that in addition to each joist being exactly level, they are all level with each other and the original first joist. This is best achieved by using a simple water level which can run around the tree trunk and any branches that may be in the way.

At this stage, as the horizonal joists start to make the supporting pattern, they each have great downward strength, but little or no sideways support. To resolve this situation, temporary off cuts of wood may be screwed between the joists to create the rigidity that will later allow the platform to be locked into position once the decking is finally completed.

The bottom of the angled bracer fits exactly into the bracket as shown.

You can now start to see the position of the platform in the tree from a distance.

One of the bottom angle brackets in place showing the small hardwood wedge.

Taking into account the temporary nature of the pieces joining the joists, we now need to mark, cut, position, and bolt up the network of joists between the main joists. Working on the first segment, make a mark on the top of each bracer starting 6″ (15cm) from the tree trunk, the next mark should be 2′ (60cm) further out and then 2′ (60cm) further until you reach the end of the bracers.

Move around to the next segment and make the first mark 9″ (23cm) out from the tree trunk and at 2′ (60cm) centers from then on. On the third segment start at 6″ (15cm) again followed by 2′ (60cm) and so on, making the infilling joists out of line with the ones in the neighboring segment, which allows the joist to

Each foundation piece of wood needs to be leveled with the others.

The first four supporting foundation joists and angle bracers are held in position by a horizontal off cut to give some lateral rigidity.

be attached to the bracers by screwing through the bracer into the end of the joists.

Next, each joist needs to be cut to size, with the correct angle cut at each end. To achieve this, a length of 2″ x 6″ (5 x 15cm), slightly longer than the measurement between the marks, needs to be cut and then lifted into place overlapping each of the two marks on the bracers and carefully marked on the underside with the required angle. Then it should be lowered to the ground to be accurately cut. It is more efficient if one person remains on the platform, marking and fixing, and the other raises and lowers and cuts to length.

As each cut section is brought back up to the tree it should be placed between the bracers, lined up with the marks, and attached by using 6″ (15cm) lag bolts through the bracer and into the end grain of the joist.

Though knee bracer brackets at differing heights may look untidy, the tree benefits from not having a ring of drill holes at one level.

Once the ten horizontal joists and knee bracers are in place, a framework of joists is built on top to give lateral rigidity.

A grid work of supporting lumber is created above the horizontal joists and 45-degree knee bracers.

The complete foundation of joists photographed before the decking process commences.

Note: Make sure that when each joist is fitted, the top of the joist is exactly flush with the top of the bracer. As you work your way around the tree, the temporary off cuts that were holding the bracers in position may be removed and discarded.

As each piece is fitted, the platform will begin to stiffen up and after a time you will begin to feel a degree of security as the base becomes firmer. This will continue to improve as the interior and exterior decking is screwed on in turn.

Carefully marking out from the plan the exact area of the treehouse interior, (including and taking into account the depth of the wall thickness), the interior flooring and exterior decking can now be put in place. Something that will help in determining the boundary of internal and external flooring is the curved plywood sole plate, which is described in detail in the next chapter.

It is vital that joists are positioned half on and half off this final area of decking. Several additional joists may now have to be carefully positioned and

A gap should be left around the trunk to allow for future growth.

The curved plywood sole plate, constructed as part of the framework, is used to check the extent of the internal floor.

The completed internal floor area viewed from below.

fitted in place at this stage to provide something to screw on to.

The interior flooring may now be fixed on, using 2½″ (6.3cm) galvanized nails and making sure that the tongue and groove joints are firmly knocked into place, either with a wooden mallet, or a block of wood with a steel hammer. (Note: no gaps are left in the internal floor area, though they are in the external decking.)

After the internal flooring is positioned, cut into shape, and fixed, the ribbed redwood flooring material may now be screwed into place. Each piece should be parallel with the last and with a ¼″ (6.3mm) gap left between each piece. This exterior decking can be left overlong and can be cut to the final shape when the platform is almost completed. Once a large enough area has been covered, you may sit or stand on the completed flooring; however, make sure you are securely fastened to the tree at all times.

Whenever a piece of flooring runs up to or across the tree trunk, it is very important that the decking is measured to leave a gap of 1½″ (3.8cm) around the trunk, allowing room for the tree to grow.

The sole plate is not fixed to the platform at this stage of the build, but it can come in handy for marking out areas.

At this stage all the temporary supporting posts may be removed. Once the site is cleared of any off cuts, you can stand back and see the platform sitting in your tree, strong and level.

The internal flooring is laid without gaps and carefully butted together with the tongue and groove joints creating the strength.

Though you will be using treated wood, it is still best to fit the internal flooring during a period of dry weather.

Once the internal flooring is complete and cut to shape using the sole plate, the external decking can be fitted around it.

Mark the wood to be cut with a pencil. Whether you make the cut on the spot or at ground level is a matter of preference.

The cut wood is married up to the internal flooring and screwed into place.

The inner sole plate has been pushed aside as the decking progresses on one side of the tree.

The completed external floor from below (left) and above. Note the outer sole plate about to be used as a template for trimming.

Above: Once the ribbed redwood decking is screwed into place, it can be trimmed into its circular form using a hand or jigsaw.

Right: The completed platform viewed from the ground, with knee bracers taking the strain.

The completed platform viewed from above, clearly showing the position of the treehouse and veranda area.

Variations

The treehouses shown below all have foundation platforms that vary in some way to the one constructed in this book. Often it is necessary to use a number of different methods of supporting and constructing the platform. Even if your tree is different to the one we are following in this book, you may well find the solution to your problem below.

A tree trunk with round (stained dark) bracers attached by bolts directly onto the tree with no brackets. This method is only suitable for smaller treehouses.

This treehouse sits on stilts in a small apple tree, and doesn't use the tree to support the foundation at all!

Another treehouse constructed in an oak tree, showing a ring of 45-degree bracers.

3″x 9″ (7 x 23cm) bracers in place, making a supporting cartwheel around the treetrunk.

A sturdy example of bracers on a double tree platform.

This very high treehouse clearly shows the bracers as well as the top bracket over running the edge of the platform with extended (shaped) joists.

Frame

The naked framework, or the treehouse before cladding.

Now that we have constructed and completed the foundations of the treehouse, we have a solid, level platform to work from. This allows us to build in a very similar way to a conventional building on the ground—with two big differences.

One, you will be working at height and therefore everything takes longer. Also, safety should still be at the forefront of your mind.

Two, it is likely that some branches or parts of the main trunk will be running through where the walls are going to be built, so you will need to build around them!

We can now start to construct the external walls and, for the first time, we will see what the actual finished treehouse will look like, high in the tree.

Safety

While there is an obvious advantage of having the treehouse platform completed it can also tend to lull you into a false sense of security. When constructing the walls, you will be working right at the edge of the platform; therefore, extreme caution must be taken.

SAFETY CHECK

• Have at least two people present at all times during this stage.

• Wear the appropriate safety equipment.

• Always use harness and rope when working on the open platform.

• Make sure that all ladders are securely tied at the top to the platform.

Key objectives

- Erect the exterior walls of the treehouse, leaving spaces and gaps for windows and doors.
- Clad the exterior of the treehouse with the finished material selected (except the rear of the tower section).
- Learn how to deal with branches coming through the walls, how to protect the tree, and at the same time make the treehouse waterproof.
- Outfit the interior of the treehouse (with the potential to add insulation).

As most of the walls are round in shape, you need to create a bottom and top plate (often referred to as the sole plate and head plate), which will create the shape and allow the framing uprights to be fitted. These plates are going to be cut from the $\frac{3}{4}''$ (19mm) plywood at a width of $4''$ (10cm), carefully positioned and cut from each sheet to keep waste to a minimum.

Keep the frame rigid and in place by using off cuts from the build.

EQUIPMENT

Essential	**Useful**
power drill	battery drill
jigsaw	table saw
handsaw	miter saw
tape measure	
spirit level	
hand tools	

MATERIALS

18—2″ x 4″ pressure treated softwood (16′ in length)
30—2″ x 3″ pressure treated softwood (12′ in length)
75—¾″ x 4″ pressure treated T & G cladding (16′ in length)
75—½″ x 4″ pressure treated T & G cladding (16′ in length)
24—½″ x 3″ pressure treated softwood (16′ in length)
6 sheets—4′ x 8′ exterior grade ply wood (¾″ in thickness)
3 square feet of ³⁄₁₆″ neoprene per branch or trunk that
    pierces the walls or roof

Cutting the curved top and bottom rails from plywood.

The second rail is cut to exactly the same shape by using the first as a template.

If you have managed to construct the platform as an exact circle, you will be able to measure out this circle on the ground, marking a double layer of plywood by using a pencil and a piece of string. If your platform did not work out as an exact circle, for the larger outer wall section you need to carefully take each piece of ply up onto the platform and mark two pieces for each section by using the platform as a template. Using the jigsaw, these circular sections need to be carefully cut out, in each case keeping each pair together.

The smaller circular plates for the tower section can be measured using the pencil and string, in this case with a radius of 3' 6" (1m). For this taller section three of each plate will be needed.

Straight plates in the same material will be required for the two sections to either side of the turret; two of each.

Note: At this stage, the bottom (sole) plates will be fitted to run across both of the doorways. These will be cut out and removed at a later date.

Once these plates are cut out and marked they can be fitted to the uprights. Cut 36 lengths of 2" x 3" (5 x 7.5cm) to the underside eaves height, in this case 6' (1.8m).

Where you actually construct the walls is very much down to personal preference. Some of my treehouse installers prefer to build on the ground and haul up the finished wall sections onto the platform, while others take up the pieces of wood and build on the platform. I think that if the tree is complex, in other words if it has many protruding branches, it is probably easier to build up on the deck. Hauling large sections up in this situation would probably result in them getting entangled, and a lot of work needs to be done where the branches run through the walls. On the other hand if only the tree trunk runs through the treehouse, it is probably easier to build on the ground.

If you lay out the plates, one on top of the other, in place on the platform, you will easily be able to see where each of the windows and doors will be fitted, and at the same time recognize any unforeseen

The straight walls are screwed into place, leaving a space for the door opening.

Above: The round wall frame starts to take shape.

complications caused by branches. All these facts should be marked clearly on the plates along with the position of all the uprights at 2′ (61cm) centers.

Note: If you can make the positioning of the windows and doors fit the markings for the uprights, you will save doubling up on material!

Once the plates are marked up, attach the uprights between both top and bottom plates by screwing through the bottom of one and the top of the other using two 3″ (7.6cm) screws in each case. Making sure that you leave ½″ (13mm) at either side of the upright when it is placed on the 4″ (10cm) plate.

Starting with one section that has no branches running through, screw the bottom (sole) plate to the outer edge of the platform with 2″ (5cm) screws and keep upright by using a temporary bracer loosely

A view from the turret looking down at the framework below. The frame now has the softwood straps inserted.

The other straight wall at the other side of the turret.

The frame detail around the tree boughs.

screwed into place. As you create more sections attach these to the platform as before and to the section next to each other with 3″ (7.6cm) screws. (For strength, fix some from one side and some from the other.)

Note: Wherever a branch runs through the wall, the plates and uprights will have to be fixed in position around it.

When the last section is screwed into its neighboring sections on both sides, the frame is complete.

Next you need to cut pieces of 2″ x 3″ (5 x 7.5cm) to fix above and below each window, creating

the space for the sizes of the windows that you have planned. This is the stage at which you need to finalize the window sill heights. You will see from the treehouse we are following that we have kept these regular at 2′ 3″ (68cm) above the floor height, apart from the one larger window which comes down to only 6″ (15.24cm) above the floor.

You will realize that we have not started to make up the windows yet, as I always feel it is a lot easier to do this once the space has been formed rather than trying to make the gap you have just created the exact size of a pre-formed window. This also allows you the flexibility to change and adapt window sizes depending upon the positions of the branches etc. The same 2″ x 3″ (5 x 7.5 cm) sections need to be fitted 6″ (15.24cm) above and below each branch, as each one runs through a wall.

At this stage our framework is round in shape at the top and bottom when it is ½″ (12.7mm) larger than the uprights but still quite angular between the uprights. The next task is to fix curved straps consisting of the ½″ x 3″ (1 x 7.5cm) softwood, horizontally around the uprights. These help make the final shape by providing the fixing point for the external and internal cladding. The first strap should sit on the bottom plate and be attached to each of the uprights with two 2″ (5cm) screws making sure that it is cut exactly to start and end halfway across an upright allowing space for the next strap to start or finish. This strap should continue right around the treehouse but this time not crossing either of the doors. The next strap should be fitted just under windowsill height, lining up with the lower piece of 2″ x 3″ (5 x 7.5cm) that you fitted as the lower edge for the windows.

The same procedure should be completed twice more above the window height and at the top of

During this stage of the construction, the treehouse will start to take on a shape, and you will start to see that all your effort was worthwhile.

Here, a small branch runs through the framing.

Using a nail gun for the infills will save you quite a lot of time.

The view into the distance can now be seen clearly from where the window will be fitted.

the walls touching against the top plate. The internal walls then need to have the same curved straps fitted at the same heights and in the same manner.

You will now see the shape of the lower part of the treehouse is well defined and ready to clad.

Before you start cladding the lower section, you need to construct the walls of the higher second floor tower in the clear space where the tree has spread its main boughs from the trunk. This starts in the same way as the first level with the floor, which is

The internal size of the treehouse is now easy to see and get a feel for. Even at this stage temporary bracers are needed.

A close-up of the softwood straps onto which the cladding—both internal and external—will be fixed.

constructed from 2″ x 6″ (5 x 15cm) lumber creating a framework between the outer edge of the lower tower walls, with the boughs of the tree acting as the main supports.

Once the second floor is in place and decked out with internal 1″ x 6″ (2.5 x 15cm) tongue and groove flooring, the tower walls can be put up in the same way as the floor below—again, remember to leave space for the small tower windows.

Note: Access to the second floor is through a trap door from below. Make sure you leave a space 2′ x 3′ (60 x 90cm) between two of the joists in a convenient position. Do not fill in this section.

I like to clad the interior and exterior next before constructing the roof, as it makes the whole structure stronger and forms a more stable base on which to work on the roof.

The skeleton of the treehouse shows the complexity of the structure you are building.

The last piece of framing before the cladding is fitted.

Note: The one exception during this process is the external cladding of the rear section to the tower, which should be left until the roof is formed.

The external ¾" x 4" (2 x 10cm) cladding is fitted vertically completely around the treehouse perimeter, starting at deck height at the front veranda of the structure and being cut 1" (2.5cm) longer around the remainder so as to fix hanging slightly over the edge around the remainder, creating an attractive shadow groove and also allowing water to run off easier.

Fix the cladding by using 1½" (46cm) galvanized nails (this is where a nail gun is very useful), making sure that you get a good fixing to each of the curved straps, especially the top and bottom plywood plate. Also ensure that the tongue and groove are well knocked together.

Obviously, spaces for windows and doors should not be clad and must be cut exactly to the size suitable to allow these to be fitted at a later date.

Where a branch runs through the wall it is important to make a judgement on the likely movement that a strong wind will create at this point. Try tying a rope to the branch as far out from the tree as possible and have a colleague pull and release on the rope from below as you watch for movement.

On a large bough close to the trunk, the movement is likely to be minimal and therefore the cladding can be cut to leave only a small space around the bough, say 2"–3" (5–7.6cm). On a smaller

Starting the process of cladding of the turret.

branch, which shows a greater movement, a large space needs to be provided, say 4″–6″ (10–15cm).

Before the external cladding is fitted around each of these boughs or branches, you need to fit a neoprene collar. This is formed by cutting a suitable length of neoprene with a sharp knife to wrap completely around the branch with a good overlap of

Varying the different color tones of the tongue and groove cladding is something that will add to the overall look.

The tongue and groove flooring and cladding needs to be pushed together well to form a solid joint.

The cladding is cut to fit around the windows.

Measure carefully around the tree branches, making sure to leave the appropriate gap.

The completed framework for the turret, giving a good view of the supporting platform that has been created.

The rear doorway is formed and clad exactly as the front door.

6″ (15cm) wider than the maximum gap that you are intending to leave around the cladding. The neoprene can then be carefully wrapped around the branch to form a tight collar and attached to the 2″ x 3″ (5 x 7.5cm) framework with 1″ (2.5cm) screws and ½″ (12.7mm) galvanized washers. The cladding is fitted over the neoprene and cut to the shape of the branch, leaving the gap as appropriate and the branch free to move surrounded by its collar. We will seal these gaps and collars at a later date when we make the final weatherproof checks.

If you have decided to insulate your treehouse, now is the time to cut and fit into place sections of 3″ (7.6cm) thick polystyrene insulation between each of the uprights. The internal ½″ x 4″ (1.2 x 10cm) cladding is fitted in exactly the same way as the external with the same gap left around the branches, which we will fill at a later time.

The completed exterior cladding looking through the window space.

Now we're ready for the interior cladding.

The interior cladding being cut to shape.

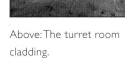

Above: The turret room cladding.

Left: The lower area of interior cladding is complete.

Variations

Because of the round shape of our treehouse, the exterior cladding is restricted to a vertical lining or cedar shingles. However, if your design is more straightforward and consists of straight walls, your choices of cladding materials are increased. Below are some other examples of possible finishes and looks that can be achieved.

A more complicated frame with an overhanging roof. This will eventually carry over the front double doors and veranda. Two large boughs run through the center of the treehouse.

The framing of a simple, square treehouse, supported by stilts and the giant sweet chestnut tree in which it is built. This is an easy frame, despite the complicated tree running through it.

A round treehouse frame on a platform with a single stilt in place for the spiral staircase. The remainder of the platform support will come from 45-degree knee bracers.

An internal view of a treehouse showing branches running through the walls. To help keep the structure rigid, larger branches are given their own specific framing.

Internal cladding where the tree limb comes through the floor and out via the wall, before rope work is completed.

Rope has been added to mask the gap that must remain to allow the tree room to grow.

Cedar shingles cladding a treehouse turret. Shapes like this can make an attractive internal desk area for a tree office.

This large, completed treehouse features cedar shingles and vertical cedar cladding in a multi-stemmed ash tree.

Roofing

The central post supports the turret roof. It will be cut out when the roof is completed.

In effect, the treehouse that we are following has two separate roofs—the turret and the surrounding "skirt" to the rear half. First, I will explain how we can form a framework to the turret using a central post for support that will later be removed, and second, how to construct the frame between the two walls of the turret and the exterior. I can then explain how to cover the roof framing with thick marine plywood to create the strength and shape before cladding with the waterproof cedar shingles.

Safety

During the construction of the roofs you will be working at the highest points of the treehouse and be most exposed to danger.

It is vital that you wear your harness at all times and never clip off your safety rope before clipping on to a second line or fixing.

SAFETY CHECK

• Have at least two people present at all times during this stage.

• Always have your safety line attached to your harness.

• Don't attempt to work on the roof section during bad weather.

• Make sure your method of accessing the roof is safe and secure.

Key objectives

• Make the framework for both roof sections.

• Cover both roofs with marine plywood.

• Clad both roofs with cedar shingles.

• Form watertight seals around the branches as they protrude through the roof.

• Seal and leave the complete roof weatherproof.

Though the framework has rigidity and strength by now, it is still best to brace it throughout the roofing process.

Starting with the turret roof, you need to create a central support around which the roof will be formed. Carefully mark the exact center of the tower on the floor and place the 4″ (10cm) post in this place, using the spirit level in its vertical mode. Make sure that this post is exactly plumb and hold in place by using bracers to the walls from off cuts.

EQUIPMENT

Essential	**Useful**
power drill	battery drill
jigsaw	bench saw
handsaw	pulley and rope
tape measure	miter saw
hammer	wooden mallet
spirit level	
hand tools	

MATERIALS

1—4″ round post (12′ in length)
48—2″ x 3″ pressure treated softwood (16′ in length)
14 sheets— 4′ x 8′ marine grade plywood (³/₄″ in thickness)
cedar roofing shingles to cover 400 square feet
15 lb bronze nails
3 square feet of ³/₁₆″ neoprene per branch or trunk that
    pierces the roof
12″ x 15′ lead sheet to form 3′ circle

The roof spars are now in place for the turret roof, and the cladding has started.

Note: The spaces left for windows will make excellent fixings to attach the bracers required.

It does not matter how much the post protrudes above the top of the roofline as this will be cut off flush when the roof is almost completed.

Using the 2″ x 3″ (5 x 7.5cm) softwood, a frame is now needed from the outer edge of the tower walls to the central post. Mark the center post with a line all the way around at the finished roof height that was established at the planning stage—in this case 24′ 4″ (7.5m) from the ground. Make a mark around the top ring on the top plywood tower wall plate at 2′ (60cm) centers. Initially from every other one of these marks, cut a length of framing material 18″ (46cm) longer than the measurement from your mark to the top height line around the central post.

Using a combination square, mark the angle you require to fit the 2″ x 3″ (5 x 7.5cm) flush to the central post and either by hand or with the miter saw, cut 10 of these. Hold one of these roof joists in place against the post and resting on the outer wall; then mark a 1″ (2.5cm) groove which will allow the joist to sit in place on the wall without support. This groove should be cut from each of the ten pieces by hand in exactly the same place. Making sure that you miss alternate markings, fix these first joists to the wall plate and to the central post equally distant with 2½″ (6.4cm) screws.

You will find that when placing another piece of the 2″ x 3″ (5 x 7.5cm) from one of the alternate marks not used with the first ten joists to the central post, that the space is restricted and that these secondary joists will not completely reach the post. Using the adjustable square, mark the angles required to create a wedge shape between the initial joists to ensure a good fit. This should be repeated ten times and when complete the first one should be placed in

The roof is covered one section at a time with ¾″ (1.9cm) plywood carefully cut to fit exactly into place and closely to the next piece.

position resting on the top wall plate and marked for the retaining groove as previously. The length of the overhang can be the same as the first joists.

The second round of joists can now be fixed into place using the same screws and the finished shape of the tower roof can now be clearly seen.

These joists have to be covered with 20 sections (which should all be identical) of ¾″ (19mm) marine ply. Taking extreme care, the measurements should be taken of one section so that only half of each of the joists will be covered, allowing the next piece also to be attached to the same joist.

The roof spars are shortened once the plywood is in place.

The roof is completely clad with 20 sections of ¾" (19mm) plywood.

Note: I recommend cutting a template for the first section from a lighter ¼" (6.4mm) plywood. This will allow it to be adjusted and marked to get it exactly right in position on the roof, and then used to mark up the required 20 pieces of ¾" (2cm) sections.

With great care and accuracy, the marine ply roof sections should all be cut. This is where the bench saw will be invaluable: a handsaw will need patience and perseverance.

Carefully taking each of these pieces up on to the roof in turn, the sections should be screwed into place with 2" (5cm) screws. The end result of this stage should be a solid roof. While made of flat panels, it should have a cone shape starting to appear. This cone will be strong enough to sit/kneel on and

the central post can make a good point to tie on any extra safety ropes for additional security.

The secondary roof is covered with the ¾" (19mm) plywood in exactly the same way as the tower, except in this case branches are protruding through the roof. The plywood therefore needs to be cut not only to fit into place between the joists but also to leave a gap, as we did with the walls around each branch. Around each of these boughs or branches, we need to form the neoprene collar in the same manner in which we did with the walls prior to starting to shingle the roof.

Starting from the very outer ring of the roof, a circle of cedar shingles should be fixed with 1" (2.5cm) bronze nails, overlapping the marine plywood

The treehouse turret is clad, as seen from a distance.

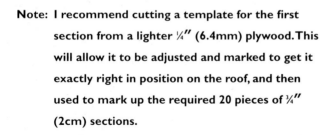

Notching the roof spars will help spread the load as they lie on the upper wall plate of the frame.

The roof spar configuration used to create the entrance overhang.

by ½″ (12.7mm). The next circle of shingles should completely cover the first layer, again with a ½″ (12.7mm) overlap and offset from the first line to always cover the gap between the first shingles laid. Each circular layer from now on should only leave 3″ (7.6cm) of the circle below uncovered and must always cover the gap between the shingles beneath.

For the first four rows, the shingles may be fixed without adjustment, but from row five upwards towards the peak, the diameter of the circle will be getting smaller and you will need to trim each shingle to an angle at the sides using a sharp knife or jigsaw to allow a good fit. This angle will become more acute as you rise up toward the top of the roof and the circle becomes tighter.

The roof and "skirt" with all the marine ply fixed in place. At bottom right is the joist arrangement for the roof of the entrance.

The plywood roof sheeting is cut out around the tree boughs leaving plenty of space.

When you have fixed shingles as high as you can with whole pieces, you will have to reduce the length of each shingle for the final three rows up to the central post. This post needs to be removed, so make sure your safety line is well attached to the tree, preferably at two separate points.

The post should be cut horizontally with a sharp handsaw ½" (12.7mm) above the level where the final shingles are fitted.

Place the lead circle centrally over the post after it has been cut. Using a soft wooden mallet work the lead around the central post to fit the shape of the post and then the roof surrounding it, overlapping the

Both roofs are now sheeted with the plywood and are ready for cladding.

Shingling commences! In this case, we have the benefit of temporary scaffolding to help speed up the job.

The shingles are started at the edge of the roof and work upwards. Note the level of overlap on each layer.

The finished effect is both rustic and attractive and will last up to 30 years without any maintenance.

Above: Shingling of the lower roof, showing the neoprene collars in place around the limbs of the tree.

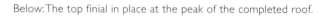

Below: The top finial in place at the peak of the completed roof.

Both roofs totally shingled and complete, with lead flashing at the base of the turret.

shingles. Using some 1½″ (38mm) galvanized clout nails, fix the lead into position.

The next step is to create a seal between the rear of the tower wall and the roof. This is the only section that we did not clad before. You need to lay the long lead strip around where the wall and roof meet below the windows. Gently form this into shape as you did with the top roof piece. Due to its long length—and great weight—it may be necessary to cut the lead into shorter sections. If this is done, make sure that they are well overlapping. Once you are

happy with the seal around this potentially vulnerable area, the cladding of the rear tower can be completed. As can be seen above, the cladding runs over the lead work.

The rear roof may now be shingled in precisely the same way as the higher tower, working up from the outside edge and finishing by tucking under the lead flashing recently formed. Only a shower of rain or a long hose pipe will prove how waterproof the roof is, but with windows and doors to fix, and final sealing to be carried out, the drier it stays the better!

Variations

The simplest variation to the cedar shingles used on this treehouse are felt shingles. They come in sheets of three or four tiles in a pack that will cover 6–8 square feet (0.5–0.7m²) and are easy to fix, fairly light in weight and very suitable for treehouse construction. They are also a lot cheaper than the natural cedar shingles; however they will not last as long and, depending on how much of the roof will be seen, probably won't look as good. Thatching also makes a good treehouse roof but is probably best left to an expert. I hope that by looking at the photos below you will see some of the variations in type and style of roof that may help you decide what you would like on your own treehouse.

Whatever roof you choose, MAKE SURE YOU ARE SAFE!

A craftsman on a roof with climbing gear.

Detail of African reed tiles on a bamboo frame.

Looking down on the frame of the roof from above.

Ridge detail of square felt shingles in green.

Another example of a neoprene collar fitted to the tree bough.

Completed African reed tiled roof with a tree trunk through the center.

A completed cedar shingle octagonal roof.

Windows and Doors

The windows and doors that will be fitted to your treehouse will affect
the overall look and style of the finished project, but they also have very
important practical considerations and implications.

It is very important that a treehouse is light and
bright inside. Too often I have visited home-built
treehouses (during my travels I can never resist a
chance to see how someone else has constructed a
treehouse), to find that the owner has skimped on
windows and the result is a dark and rather dreary
interior. When you are up a tree, you should be able
to see that you are in the branches, and the ground
far below and as many windows as possible should be
fitted to let any available light stream in. Remember
that the tree canopy will also reduce light, so the more
chance you have of catching it the better. In our treehouse there are eight windows!

You will notice from the design elevations that
there are smaller windows in the turret to keep the
proportions correct and larger ones below. There was
also one special request from our client's oldest
child—she wanted a long window, right down to the
treehouse platform. The reason for this is that she
wanted to sleep in the treehouse and be able to lie in
her sleeping bag and look straight out to see how high
she was above the ground and watch the birds and
tree animals from their own height. We made sure
we adapted this request into the design.

We have intentionally left the construction of
the windows and doors until the treehouse walls are
complete and the exact dimensions and shapes of the
windows and doors are known. Even with the best
planning it is very easy to end up with different sizes
and shapes of windows as you progress through the
initial stages of the treehouse construction.

I also often find that while the windows look
adequate during the planning stage, I add a window
or two while building the walls to catch a special view
that I was not aware of earlier, or an unusual shape of
window to cope with a branch I had not anticipated!

The other functionality of the windows is to let
in fresh air; however this has to be set against the
aspect of safety. Where possible I try to design treehouses where the windows that open are only placed
over a balcony or veranda, but this very much
depends on who is going to be using the treehouse.
For a treehouse office, for example, I would probably
have all the windows able to be opened.

Depending on where the treehouse is to be
sited, security may be a consideration. If located
away from your home—at the bottom of a field or
near a public trail—a treehouse is bound to attract
attention. Even the most well-behaved child is likely
to try the door of such an inviting "den," so good
locks on the doors and windows may be necessary,
depending on the location.

Other treehouse visitors are also likely,
except they were probably on-site before the treehouse was even considered. Birds and squirrels are
bound to be drawn to explore a treehouse, especially
if food is left about and windows and doors are left
open, so good window and door catches will also

reduce any likelihood of damage from other potentially troublesome tree-dwellers.

Safety

Most of the work involved in the construction of the windows and doors will be done on the ground, so the main area of concern is with tool safety. Even when fitting the windows and doors, you now have a solid platform and surrounding walls, so the safety aspect is less critical than all the previous phases. Still take care, though, and don't rush.

SAFETY CHECK

• Make sure that you always use the appropriate safety clothing when using power tools and machinery.

EQUIPMENT

Essential	Useful
power drill	battery drill
handsaw	router
tape measure	miter saw
spirit level	bench saw
block plane	electric planer

MATERIALS

8—2″ x 3″ pressure treated structural softwood (12′ in length)
8—2″ x 4″ pressure treated structural softwood (16′ in length)
16—¾″ x 1″ pressure treated softwood (12′ in length)
9—¾″ x 4″ T & G boarding (16′ in length)
doubleglazed *toughened* window units made to measure
        or 36 square feet polycarbonate (¼″ in thickness)
door and window, latches, hinges, and fittings

Key objectives

- Construct the windows to fit.
- Construct the door frames and doors.
- Decorate some of the windows with leading and colored glass.
- Hang the door frame and doors.
- Fit the windows.
- Fit the window and door hardware.

Before starting to make up the windows, you need to decide what to fit them with; the decision is often dependent on the tree itself and its likely movement, and also the required use of the treehouse once it is finished.

In the case of the treehouse we are following, a doubleglazed, toughened unit has been selected. We can do this because the oak tree in which we are building is very large and the movement that will occur within the treehouse, solidly anchored to the huge trunk, will be minimal. Also, the additional weight of the doubleglazed units will not be significant in a tree of this size, and because the intention is to use the treehouse all year round, the additional insulation will be useful.

Note: Never use single sheet or non-toughened glass in a treehouse.

However, if the tree you are building in is smaller and less mature, and if you have seen significant movement of the trunk or main boughs, you should opt for the safer ¼″ (6mm) polycarbonate. This material is incredibly strong and almost impossible to break, even when forced to flex in high winds. It obviously does not have the insulation qualities of a doubleglazed unit, but it is lighter and cheaper. Its main drawback is that it tends to scratch quite easily. If you are not sure which to use, go for the polycarbonate. You can cut it to size yourself, so that you can have it on site at the beginning of the construction, whereas the doubleglazed units will have to be ordered when you have the exact sizes.

Constructing the doors and windows for the flat walls is a fairly simple exercise; the curved walls, however, require a bit more thought and effort.

Carefully measure the size of the aperture that you have left for each window and check that these are square by measuring across the angles—they should both be the same. For the windows on the flat walls, the external and internal sizes will both be the same, but with the windows and doors on the round walls you will find that the internal measurement is slightly less than the external.

Spaces left in cladding for windows; in this instance, a full-length window is being fitted alongside a standard size window.

Completed windows ready to be fitted.

With the frames in place, but the windows and doors absent, the treehouse takes on a slightly haunted ambience.

Although there are many ways to make a window, I would suggest a simple frame with 45-degree mitered corners, glued and screwed, with separate mullions to hold the glass or polycarbonate.

Cut your 2″ x 3″ (5 x 7.5cm) to the exact size of each of the four sides of each window in each case with an exact 45-degree miter; this is where a good miter saw will be invaluable.

Holding two pieces together at an exact right angle, pre-drill the frame through one angle into the other. Coat one angled surface with a good-quality wood glue and then firmly screw the two pieces together with 3″ (7.6cm) screws, making sure that the screw head is buried well into the frame. Repeat this process with the other two sides until you have a solid

rectangle. Check that this is absolutely square by measuring across the corners, and then put it to one side for the glue to dry.

The eight mullions, two for each side, should be cut from the ½″ x 1″ (1 x 2.5cm) wood to fit exactly inside the window frame, again with a 45-degree angle miter. At this stage, before the glazing is fixed, I prefer to stain the window frame and mullions, as it is a lot easier on the ground and I don't have to worry about staining the glazing. Normally I like to create a contrast with the color of the windows, and in this case we have selected a dark green stain/preserver (the wood is already pressure treated, but another coat of a stain that also acts as a preservative will certainly do no harm). The choice of colors is completely up to the prospective owner, but I would suggest you keep it to a natural green or brown.

If you are intending to decorate the glass or polycarbonate, now is the time to do so. Attractive leading makes any window stand out and the use of colored films to create a stained glass look is extremely effective in a treehouse, where the light tends to be dappled between the leaves. Rolls of stick-on leading and stained-glass film are available in most good hardware stores.

The secret of good lead work and stained glass is keeping the surface of the glass clean. This is one of the few jobs during the construction of the treehouse that is best carried out indoors; it is an ideal job for a day of bad weather.

When you have decided on the design you require, draw it on a paper template for each size of window that you are planning to install. Using this template, mark the stained glass film and cut it to size. Peel it off the backing sheet and carefully apply it to the correct place on the glass. The leading is applied in the same way to cover the edges of the film and give the impression that you have a genuine stained-glass window.

Note: Where two pieces of lead cross, mold them together with a blunt knife. If you do not want the shiny look of new lead and would prefer it to look aged, wipe it with a light acid solution such as vinegar.

Once the stain has dried, the first set of mullions can be pinned and glued into place, leaving space for the doubleglazed unit or polycarbonate to be positioned centrally. Before placing the units or plastic sheet into place, run a thin bead of clear silicon around the inside edge of the mullion and gently squeeze the glazing onto this. The second set of mullions should have a similar layer of silicon and glue on the corresponding sides (silicon against glass, glue against wood) before they are carefully put in place and pinned permanently.

The windows prepared for the flat walls should now be ready to be fitted and screwed directly into place. However, the windows that are to fit into the curved walls will need more work. Mark on one side of the window frame the smaller internal measurements that you took earlier; the frame needs to be trimmed down at an angle to this size. This can be simply done with the bench saw set at the correct angle or with careful use of an electric plane. A bench plane will achieve the same result but will take a lot longer. Keep trying the window in place until you get an exact fit, at which point the window can be screwed into place. A thin wooden frame will create a neat finish if carefully fitted around the windows both internally and externally.

Unlike the windows, the doors require a separate frame to be fitted into place between the existing uprights. This is also the stage when the bottom plywood plate that was left in place when the walls were fitted can be removed. Carefully cut through each side of the plate and, after unscrewing any fixings, lift the plate and discard it.

Windows fitted in place showing the simple stained glass.

The frame is made by cutting three pieces of the 3″ x 4″ (7.5 x 10cm) to the same sizes as both the sides and the top of the opening and screwing them into place with 4″ (10cm) screws.

The doors are constructed in much the same way as the windows with an additional central wood support for strength and, if you are sufficiently confident, a mortise and tennon joint rather than the simple 45-degree miter you made for the windows. Once the frame is constructed and the glue dried the door should be clad vertically on the outer face with the ½″ x 4″ (1 x 10cm) tongue-and-groove boarding. A weatherboard fashioned from an angled off cut should be attached to the bottom edge of the door.

At this stage the door can be stained to match the walls or the window frames.

Fitting the pre-stained windows carefully into place.

In this instance, the window opens out onto a veranda.

The window in place, complete with unstained frame.

When dry, the doors can be hung with four galvanized butt hinges and the appropriate door hardware, lock, and handles fitted.

You can achieve stained glass effects cheaply and easily. Leading strips will weather quickly to give the treehouse a lived-in look.

Never be afraid to add extra windows as the project unfolds and new vistas present themselves.

The specially requested full-length picture window.

Variations

The shape and style of the windows and doors can make
a big difference to the overall look of your treehouse.
Some of the versions shown below may give you ideas.

A large, floor-level, four-sided
window with four panels (two
triangles) giving loads of light.

Window frame in place before the glazing is fitted,
with a rough-edged wooden cladding.

Simple, square fixed four-pane windows and
square door from inside the treehouse.

An arched door with a small arched window in the door and an
arched window next to it, at a lower level, for children to enjoy.

Top opening windows in an attractive treehouse. The top lights
have stick-on diamond leaded glass. The door is square, with an
arched leaded glass top section.

An arched window with leaded glass.

A square framed window and door, both frames stained dark green. The door is stenciled with leaves and flowers.

A round window surrounded with thick rope gives an extra nautical feel by the plywood ship's wheel, cut to fit.

An arched door with castle-style fittings.

An extended window acting as a recessed window seat. It has six panes, created with narrow wooden mullions; the whole surrounded with cedar shingles.

Railings

The prime function of a railing around the edge of a veranda or balcony, or on either side of a staircase, is safety. It is vital that the finished railing will be able to support several people leaning against it at the same time, or a child, for example, falling or being pushed against it—or even running into it at top speed.

Remember that a treehouse is likely to generate excited play, so don't be tempted to take shortcuts when constructing the railings.

As well as ensuring safety, the railings will add to the overall appearance of the treehouse and therefore needs to be considered for its aesthetic suitability as well as its strength. The railings used on this treehouse are strong and functional, yet because they are fitted in a slightly random fashion give a less formal look than if fitted vertically and evenly.

Safety

Once again you will be working at the edge of the platform and therefore should be tied on with your harness at all times.

We will mention the importance of annual maintenance at the end of this book, but it is important to point out at this stage that the railings should be checked individually at least once a year to make sure that they are still strong and adequate.

SAFETY CHECK

• **Make sure that you are tied on at all times.**

• **Ensure that the finished railings are strong and suitable for their purpose.**

• **Don't fix the rails horizontally between the posts as this will encourage children to climb on them.**

Key objectives

• Construct a safe and attractive set of railings around the large front veranda.
• Form railings around the rear platform.
• Create a safety gap over the rope ladder access.
• Build a simple gate to protect the zip slide exit.

The strength for our treehouse railings comes from the main supporting posts, which are made from 4″ (10cm) diameter round posts. The posts need to sit flush against the main 2″ x 8″ (5 x 20cm) support joists and be strongly bolted through these joists.

Around the edge of the veranda, mark exactly where the edge of each of the main foundation wood pieces lie, 5″ (12.5cm) in from the outside edge.

Note: **The easy way to do this is by using a long thin drill bit from the underside; after marking 5″ (12.5cm) in from the outer edge right next to the 2″ x 8″ (5 x 20cm) lumber, drill upward and through the decking.**

Next prepare the 4″ (10cm) posts. Cut each 16′ (5m) post into four pieces, each 4′ (1.2m) in length. At one

EQUIPMENT

Essential	Useful
power drill	battery jigsaw
jigsaw	battery drill
handsaw	bench saw
tape measure	
spirit level	

MATERIALS

3—4″ diameter round posts, pressure treated (16′ in length)
8—2″ x 3″ pressure treated redwood (16′ in length)
16—2″ round doweling, pressure treated (12′ in length)

end of each of these posts mark a line around 9″ (22cm) from the end and at the same end mark a straight line across the bottom, 1″ (2.5cm) in from the outer edge.

By carefully cutting out the smaller 1″ x 9″ (2.5 x 22cm) rounded section, you are creating a flat side that will be bolted flush onto the underside beam. By using the prepared ends of the posts as templates, you can position these centrally over the marks you made

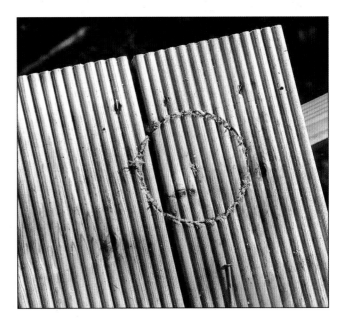

Preparing to cut the holes for the railing posts.

Above: The cut bottom end of the railing post will fit through the hole and butt up flush against the joist below, allowing for a very sturdy joint.

Right: During the fitting of the railing try to keep the veranda clear of debris; it makes working a lot easier.

Left: The railing posts fitted into place. You can drill the holes for the top and bottom rail before fixing them.

Top and bottom rails fitted to the upright posts.

A screw gun will dramatically cut this job down to size.

The dowels are deliberately angled to give a home-built quality to what is a professionally constructed treehouse.

Each post should now be strong and will not move when you try to push against it.

The 2″ x 3″ (5 x 7.5cm) poles make up the top and bottom rails which should be fixed to the inside of the posts. Measure between each of the posts and cut two pieces of lumber for each section. Make two marks 6″ (15cm) and 26″ (66cm) from the top of each post and line up the corresponding pieces of 2″ x 3″ (5 x 7.5cm) with these marks, fixing with two 4″ (10cm) screws at each end.

Note: Do not fix wood across the opening that will have the rope ladder attached.

Cut 60 pieces of the 2″ (5cm) round dowel at 32″ (81cm) length. When fixing the round dowels to the top and bottom rails keep the same height—4″ (10cm)—from the deck all the way around, but vary the vertical angle of each of the railings. (Unless you want a picket fence effect in which case keep them all vertical.) Fix each rail with a 3″ (7.5cm) screw into both rails, top and bottom, making sure that no gap is more than 6″ (15cm) wide at any place on the veranda.

As noted above, do not attach railings to the section between which the rope ladder will be fixed. Instead cut two lengths of 2″ (5cm) dowel from one of the remaining pieces and fix with two 6″ (15cm) lag bolts to the posts at either side of the rope ladder gap. The bottom rail will create a final grab handle when climbing up or down the ladder and the top rail will act as a safety bar.

The railings to the small rear deck are fitted in exactly the same manner, though here a small gate will be made to protect the area from where the cable slide will take off. It is best to have a gate to protect the cable slide exit point, because it cannot have a safety rail. A small lock can be fitted to stop the cable slide being used by children without supervision.

on the decking and draw around them. Using a jigsaw carefully cut out the shape taking care not to cut into the main support beam below.

The post can then be placed in the hole and should sit upright by itself, unable to drop through because of the lip, and supported by the decking. Make sure the post is exactly perpendicular by using the spirit level in its vertical position. Drill two ½″ (13mm) holes through the post below the decking and continue straight through the foundation joist. Each post can now be bolted to the frame with ½″ x 6″ (13 x 150mm) lag bolts, making sure you use larger 1″ (2.5cm) washers on each side as well as lock nuts.

The gate is fixed between two of the round posts and made up simply from two pieces of the 2″ x 3″ (5 x 7.5cm) cut slightly wider than the gap size and 2″ (5cm) dowel cut to 32″ (81cm) again and screwed randomly between the top and bottom rail.

Note: **On a simple gate like this, glue the pieces to add extra strength. The gate will probably get a lot of use, as zip slides are popular.**

When solid, the gate can be hung with a pair of galvanized butt hinges and a latch (sometimes called a Suffolk latch). I also like these to be painted as well.

Completed early on, railings can improve the safety on a build; but make sure they don't block the movement of materials.

This side gate is used to keep smaller children out of the zip slide area.

The completed railings around the front veranda provide a strong and decorative surround.

Variations

While safety is the most important consideration when it comes to the railings, your choice will dramatically affect the look of the treehouse.

Note: With all railings make sure you leave a gap under the bottom rail to allow the veranda to be swept off, nothing is worse for wood than to have a build-up of wet leaves lying for long periods of time. Do not fix the bottom rail to the decking as this will collect water and debris.

Many materials can be used to create interesting and eye-catching railings. Some of the best that I use on a regular basis are:

Twigs and branches cut from trees during routine pruning and left to dry before soaking in preservative. With care, a veranda surrounded with these most natural of materials looks superb, but it does take a lot of work and preparation.

Square sectioned 2″ x 2″ (5x5cm), makes for a rather formal balcony rail but this can be quite suitable in some treehouses.

Rope twisted round and over wooden top and bottom rails and then screwed into place. If you do decide to use rope, make sure you use a 1″ (2.5cm) washer over the heads of the screws and use round top and bottom rails rather than square.

Flat sections of 1″ x 3″ (2.5 x 7cm) with a shaped (normally rounded) top fixed vertically.

Bamboo balcony rails make an interesting and ornate set of railings. Always pre-drill bamboo before screwing otherwise it will split.

Sticks and branches soaked in preservative, drilled and then fitted, giving a natural look.

Criss-cross rope railings are great for taking advantage of distant views, though care should be taken with small children.

Simple mop-stick railings attached to a mop-stick top and bottom rail.

Outward sloping posts with four horizontal rails. These railings are not suitable for a treehouse used by young children.

Left: Willow hurdle used as railings.

Right: Another version of simple railings with 1″ x 3″ (2.5 x 7cm) cut to length, with a shaped top and screwed or bolted to the outside of top and bottom rails.

Right: A different angle on the sloping railings seen above. Apart from allowing small children to fall between the rails, they are a great temptation to climb.

A more complex set of railings constructed from shaped pieces of plywood cut with a jigsaw.

A bamboo railing. Thin stalks of bamboo are drilled and inset into a thicker bamboo top and bottom rail, with rope detail at the posts.

Ladders and Staircases

The method of access and exit from your treehouse needs careful thought and, as discussed in the chapter on planning, is quite dependent upon who will be using the treehouse. If purely for children over the age of seven years, a ladder may be more appropriate and appear more adventurous. However, if the treehouse is to be used as an office, where bulky furniture and computers are going to be required, a wide staircase will be more appropriate.

If a ladder is going to be the only method of entry and exit I strongly suggest using a double rung ladder. This simple ladder creates a larger footprint with both rails being used by the feet, while still allowing smaller hands to grip easily around the front rail. I believe this type of ladder is the most suitable for all treehouses.

While a rope ladder at first appears to be a great idea, I don't think it should be used as the only method of climbing in and out of the treehouse. Rope ladders are difficult to use and almost impossible for the very young or the older generation. If you do decide that a rope ladder will be the only mode of access, make sure it can be clipped to a solid peg firmly driven into the ground, which will make it much easier to use. When unclipped it can still be pulled up after you, which is one of its great attractions.

With a traditional staircase, for safety I suggest that you do not make a single stair run more than 12 stairs in length without a change of direction and a small landing.

In this case, the treehouse is intended for the entire family, and we decided that a simple double staircase would be made and fitted, as well as a simple double rung ladder from the lower floor into the higher turret room and also a rope ladder from the front veranda to the ground. However, at the end of this chapter for the more adventurous, there is some advice on how to construct a spiral staircase.

EQUIPMENT

Essential

power drill
handsaw
tape measure
spirit level
hand tools
jigsaw

Useful

battery drill
pulley and rope
bench saw
wooden mallet

MATERIALS

12—2″ x 10″ pressure treated structural softwood (16′ in length)
1—2″ x 6″ pressure treated softwood (16′ in length)
2—2″ x 4″ pressure treated redwood (12′ in length)
12—1″ diameter, pressure treated round doweling (12′ in length)
6—1½″ x 6″ treated ribbed redwood decking (14′ in length)
32—steel L-shaped galvanized angle brackets
6—5″ diameter, pressure treated round posts
1″ diameter, natural fiber rope (30′ in length)
binding string

Safety

The main wood pieces required for the staircase are even larger than the main foundations; therefore special care must be taken when lifting these. Safety gloves and especially safety boots must be worn.

Constructing the staircase at this stage of the treehouse build is quite intentional; the walls and railings of the treehouse are now complete, making a safe environment for any visitors. While a staircase may have been very useful during the earlier build program, I strongly believe that you should not make this an easy and tempting access point until the treehouse is safe in case children or visitors are tempted to climb up while you are not around.

If you do install the staircase or ladder early in the construction program, make sure that it is well taped off when you leave the site for the day, preferably with a red and white barrier tape and a large

Above and above right: The bottom posts of the staircase are placed on a concrete block and cemented into place.

SAFETY CHECK

• **Make sure that you use the appropriate safety equipment.**

• **Make sure you have someone else available to help you lift heavy lumber.**

• **Do not have a staircase of more than 12 treads without a change of direction and a small landing.**

• **Allow the rope ladder to be clipped to the ground to make climbing easier and safer.**

sign saying "No Entry." I cannot stress enough that you may know which parts of the treehouse are safe and ready for use, but no one else will and children will want to use the treehouse to play no matter if it is completed or not. Take care when you are not at the treehouse—this is when accidents are most likely to happen.

Key objectives

- To construct an easy to use two-way staircase up and onto the rear veranda.
- To build a double rung ladder from the main treehouse into the higher tower room.

Central posts fitted in place.

The first step in constructing the main staircase is to install the 5″ (12.7cm) posts at the base. While the concrete for these is setting, the double rung ladder can be made and fitted.

Your plan should clearly show the exact location of each of the posts, so mark the position and dig a hole 18″ (45cm) in diameter and at least 3′ (1m) deep. Build a 2″ (5cm) high square wall around the top of this hole with off cuts lightly screwed together. This frame will allow the concrete to be filled slightly higher than the surrounding ground and therefore protect the exposed foot of the post (its weakest point) from lying water. Spread the base of this hole with a 2″ (5cm) layer of gravel and compact this. I then like to lay into the hole a 12″ (30cm) paving slab making sure that it is level. Place each of the posts centrally onto these slabs and support them in an exactly perpendicular position using some off cuts, screwed into a triangle, to brace them on the ground. Carefully, and without disturbing the post, pour in a strong concrete mix of 40 parts cement, 40 parts sharp building sand and 20 parts fine gravel/small stone. When half full, tap down on the wet concrete all around the post to release any trapped air and make sure the entire void is filled. Continue to fill until the mixture completely fills the hole and rises approximately 1″ (2.5cm) above ground level within the temporary frame. Leave to set for a few hours and then remove the wooden frame. With a trowel gently trim away some of the semi-hardened mixture to tidy up the footing and make a slight slope away from the post in all directions. The post should then be left to set for two days after which the post bracers can be removed.

While waiting for the concrete to completely harden you can make the double rung ladder. Measure the distance from the floor of the treehouse to the opening you have left in the first floor ceiling at an angle of about 60 degrees. Cut two pieces of the 2″ x 4″ (5 x 10cm) making each piece 4″ (10cm) longer than you have measured, then trim the bottom of both legs to the angle that corresponds with the angle up into the higher floor area. Mark with a straight line across each of the legs, evenly, at spaces of 10″ (25cm) at exactly the same angle as you have trimmed the ends level. At 2″ (5cm) in from both

The railings are fitted around the central platform.

edges of this line, mark the center point for two 1″ (2.5cm) diameter drill holes, and on each line bore the two holes to a depth of 1″ (2.5cm).

Note: Wrap a piece of electrical tape around the drill bit at a depth of one inch and use this as a guide to keep each drill depth the same.

Cut the correct number of 1″ (2.5cm) diameter dowel treads, each 1′ 9″ (53cm) wide. Starting on one side only, put a small amount of glue into each hole and gently hammer—using a wooden mallet or hammer and wooden block— each dowel into its hole.

Note: Make sure that each dowel is completely inserted by checking the length, and also that it is absolutely square. This will make the next stage of fitting the second side a lot easier.

Put a small amount of glue into each hole on the second side and lie it on a flat solid surface with the holes facing up. With two other people helping have them hold both ends of the side with the dowels already

Completed staircase from above.

inserted over the side on the ground, then carefully line up each dowel and gently tap the side into place. Work from one end to another, do not try to drive the dowel home at one end and ignore the other. If you take your time and constantly work up and down, this job will take far less time than if you try and rush it. Make sure the ladder is square and lie it down to let the glue dry.

When it is dry, shape the top ends of the 2″ x 4″ (5 x 10cm) into rounded handles with a jigsaw and sand them smooth. Place the ladder into position and use 6″ (15cm) screws to screw both legs to the floor and both side rails into the frame of the gap left in the floor above.

Back on to the main staircase. At a height of 6′ (1.8m) on the four central posts, mark a level line. Cut four pieces of 2″ x 6″ (5 x 15cm), each 3′ 6″ (1m) long and attach in a square around the posts with two 8″ (20cm) lag bolts at each end. This platform can now be decked with the 1½″ x 6″ (3.8 x 15cm) ribbed

decking as you did the main veranda, remembering to leave a ¼″ (6mm) gap between each board.

The first flight of stairs is created by leaning two pieces of the 2″ x 10″ (5 x 25cm) on their edges from the bottom stair post on to the newly formed central landing. Mark the ground angle on each of the sidepieces and cut off the excess with a handsaw. Putting both back into position, mark the top angle so that the sidepieces will lie, when cut, against the decking and 6″ (15cm) side frame. Cut these angles as marked and fix into position, making sure they are exactly parallel, with 4″ (10cm) and 6″ (15cm) screws to the bottom posts and the top frame.

Measure the length of the sidepiece and, dividing this into eleven, mark ten horizontal lines on the inside of both sides. With 1½″ (3.8cm) screws fix the angled steel brackets to line up with these lines. These will then support the stair treads. Cut 10 treads from 2″ x 10″ (5 x 25cm) at the exact width required to fit neatly between the two side pieces and place the

Spiral staircase with metal tread supports.

The completed double rung ladder.

A spiral staircase from below.

A good example of a spiral staircase with round stilts and, in this case, round posts used as 45-degree bracers.

treads into position, evenly resting on the angle steels. Fix into position from below with 1″ (2.5cm) screws.

The second section of stairs is constructed in exactly the same way, except you will need help to hold the sections in place as you mark them this time.

The railings can now be fitted, as in the previous section, between the posts that you have constructed. Once the posts are cut down to a standard height, the same as the veranda posts, then the staircase is ready to use.

Also shown in this chapter are different styles of stairs and ladders. Without doubt the most popular is the spiral staircase. This is rather more difficult to construct and should only be attempted by those with excellent woodworking skills..

The stairs revolve around a central 8″ (20cm) post that is concreted into place slightly deeper than the posts described above. Around this post is dug a circular trench to a nominal depth of 2′ (60cm) at a 3′ 6″ (1m) radius from the center. 2″ x 10″ (5 x 25cm) stair treads are cut to length at 3′ 9″ (114cm) and a 1″

(2.5cm) hole is bored through the center of one end, 2″ (5cm) from the end.

Working up the central post, a round gate ring (commonly used for hanging farm gates) is drilled and inserted into the post at a height of 8″ (20cm) from the ground. The end of the tread with the hole is positioned above the ring and bolted to it with a 1″ x 3″ (2 x 7.5cm) lag bolt, the other end is supported by a post which stands in a gravel bed in the previously prepared trench. By working in even steps upward and bolting one end of the tread to the central post and the other to two upright posts, one front and one back, the spiral will start to take shape.

When the last tread can be bolted to the underside of the treehouse foundation, all the posts are then cut back to a standard height and a thick rope railing screwed at two heights is placed as a handrail.

When complete, the trench is backfilled with concrete. No one is allowed to use the stairs for a couple of days while the concrete sets hard.

Variations

A simple single rung ladder connecting a lower treehouse deck to a higher lookout.

Two steps from the treehouse platform deck lead into the open door of the treehouse.

A rather unusual pink colored treehouse showing a spiral staircase with rope handrail. Two of our clients' children are on the rope ladder.

A closeup of a stair type ladder made with decking screwed between 2" × 6" side pieces, with small blocks spacing a mop stick handrail slightly above.

A closeup of a three rope handrail on a spiral staircase.

The gap for a bamboo ladder left between bamboo handrails.

A double rung staircase looking up to a crow's nest lookout.

Rope Bridges

While there is no rope bridge on the particular treehouse we are building, they are so popular that I will describe how they are constructed. I would suggest that the maximum length of a rope bridge, constructed as described below, should be up to 30′ (9m).

If you are proposing to install a rope bridge then you will probably wish to build a tree deck. In effect a tree deck is the same as the platform of your treehouse, although normally a lot smaller and completely decked with the exterior ribbed decking material. The railing should match the treehouse. A very good idea is to have a separate access, such as a rope ladder up onto the tree deck, as well as the staircase into the treehouse itself.

Safety

Spanning between two points, often quite high above the ground, requires special consideration during the construction, as well as during everyday use. Always fix a fail-safe to every rope bridge. If for any reason the chain used to provide the strength of the structure fails, a steel cable inserted for back up will comfortably support the rope bridge and anyone crossing.

Safety Check

• **Have at least two people present at all times while building a rope bridge.**

• **Always fit a safety back up system.**

Key objectives

• To construct a simple rope bridge between two trees 10 feet (3m) apart.

At the correct height for the rope bridge, carefully fix three vertical packers made from 2″ x 4″ (5 x 10cm) lumber, each 2′ (60cm) long around the rear of each tree. These should be attached with 6″ (15cm) stainless steel screws.

The purpose of these packers is to keep the chain and cable away from the trunk of the tree, to avoid cutting and harming the tree.

At its halfway point, take the chain around one of the tree trunks and hold it in place centrally on the 2″ x 4″ (5 x 10cm) with 8″ (20cm) stainless steel lag screws, put through the wood and into the tree.

With the two free ends of the chain in place on either side of the other tree, pull the chain taught.

This can be accomplished with a willing band of helpers and the chain attached to a pulling rope or, very carefully, using a pulley mounted on a four-wheel drive truck.

EQUIPMENT

Essential

power drill

handsaw

tape measure

Useful

battery drill

MATERIALS

5—1½″ x 6″ treated ribbed redwood decking (16′ in length)

⅜″ diameter, galvanized steel cable (30′ in length)

galvanized high tensile chain with a ¾″ link (30′ in length)

3″ diameter natural fiber rope (24′ in length)

½″ diameter rope (200′ in length)

When the chains are as taught as possible they can be fastened together with bolts and then coach screwed into position as previously mentioned.

Cut the ribbed decking into 4′ (1.2m) lengths and 4″ (10cm) in from each end drill two ½″ (12mm) holes, ensuring that the holes are positioned apart the same distance as three or five links of the chain.

Note: The number of spaces between links must allow two links on the same horizontal plane to be bolted to the decking boards.

Position your first board over the chains and insert two 2″ (5cm) bolts through one side of the board. Through two links of the chain, tighten these up below using 1″ (2.5cm) washers and locking nuts.

Widen or narrow the second chain and insert another two bolts and tighten as before. Repeat this procedure with the second board, leaving a gap of one link between the boards, then continue across the whole bridge.

Take the ⅜″ (9.5mm) cable and thread this through all the unused links below the rope bridge, then take the end of the cable and wrap it around the first tree, again protecting the trunk with the upright packers, and return it again through each of the chain links at the other side of the boards.

At the rear of the second tree, the cables should be joined together with three bulldog clips.

The large rope is positioned 3′ (1m) above each side of the rope bridge and attached to posts on the treehouse veranda or tree deck.

The smaller thin rope is then wrapped over and under the thick rope as well as the chain and steel cable between the decking boards and bound with binding string, to keep it tightly in position.

This view of the underside of a rope bridge shows the wooden decking boards bolted through the high tensile chain.

A rope bridge showing string bindings at top and bottom of each upright piece of rope to keep it in position.

A long rope bridge at the top of a sycamore, with a ship's wheel on the deck making it feel like a boat moving in the wind.

A rope bridge fixed between bamboo poles.

A long rope bridge between a tree deck, where access is via a wide spiral staircase, and the treehouse behind.

This rope bridge crosses the edge of a lake from the treehouse to the tree deck.

Finishing Touches

Structurally, your treehouse is now complete, and from a distance it should look extremely impressive. Closer up, however, a critical eye will spot a lot more work that needs to be done.

Safety

During this stage of the construction you will be going back up on the roof for the final time taking down the safety ropes; therefore you need to be tied on with your harness and use extreme caution.

You also need to take extra care when using a jigsaw to cut the large foundation wood pieces to their final shape.

SAFETY CHECK

- **Have at least two people present while you are working on the roof.**
- **Exercise special caution when using power tools at a height.**
- **Make sure that no one is working below when shaping the large foundation wood pieces.**

In many respects, this is the most enjoyable stage where you can take your time and get things just right.

The two main outstanding priorities are to make sure the treehouse is watertight and to stain the construction to its final colors. But before these two important jobs are done, there are a few smaller finishing touches that will make a big difference to the overall look.

Key objectives

- Shape the foundation wood pieces.
- Angle and even off the exposed roof joists.
- Fix the external door and window casings and seal.
- Add the top ornamental roof finial.
- Seal the neoprene collars, roof and walls.
- Paint all exposed metal work.
- Stain the foundation, deck, railing and walls.

The best way to cut the ends of the foundation wood pieces that have been left over length is to cut a standard template from a thin plywood scrap. Measure the overhang of all of the foundation wood pieces to establish the shortest, as this will give you the guide to the maximum standard overhang.

Cut a piece of plywood 8″ (20cm) deep and slightly shorter than the shortest overhang you have measured. Now draw a simple shape at one end of the plywood (using a paint can to draw a quarter of a circle and finishing off with a right angle corner works well, but you can draw whatever you think looks good). Cut this shape out with a jigsaw and sand smooth.

Using this template mark all of the overhanging foundation wood pieces by placing the flat end in line with the decking and marking the shape clearly on the 2″ x 8″ (5 x 20cm).

The ends of the foundation timbers are still left hanging over at this stage.

The roughly shaped foundation wood piece with the template above, before sanding.

EQUIPMENT

Essential	Useful
power drill	battery drill
jigsaw	battery jigsaw
handsaw	
hammer	
tape measure	
spirit level	
paint brushes and pots	

MATERIALS

3—½″ x 3″ pressure treated molded facings (12′ in length)
5—½″ x 1″ pressure treated facings (16′ in length)
stain
rope
sealant

Above: The finished ends of the foundation joists, together with the cut off roof joists at an angle.

Note: Mark the template shape on both sides of the 2″ x 8″ (5 x 20cm). A jigsaw blade seldom runs straight and level when cutting thick wood and it will usually need cutting from both sides.

Work your way around the treehouse shaping each of the overhanging wood pieces, taking extreme care

Adding a molding to the internal cladding.

when the off cuts fall to the ground. Several of these may be quite large and very heavy.

Next, measure each of the protruding roof joists, remembering that in the case of this treehouse you not only have the joists that surround the main roof but the tower roof as well. Again you are looking to establish the measurement of the shortest joist, as this will become your standard. Once you have found the shortest length, work around both roofs marking the length to be cut. I prefer to cut these roof joists at a slight angle in toward the roof to avoid having a sharp edge that could potentially be a hazard for a tall person. Each of the joists can then be cut to the standard length and angled with a sharp handsaw.

The windows and doors were made to have a good fit, but even the best craftsman will find small gaps where drafts and even water could find its way through. Seal completely around each window and door, between the frame and the wall, with a clear flexible silicon sealant before fixing a cover plate over the joint.

Next, cut three lengths of ½″ x 3″ (12 x 76mm) with a mitered 45-degree joint at the top of both sides to go around the two sides and across the top of each door covering about 1″ (2.5cm) of the frame and 2″ (5cm) of the external cladding, fix these with 2″ (5cm) galvanized nails. In exactly the same way with the windows, after sealing the joint cut four pieces of ½″ x 1″ (12 x 25mm) each with mitered 45-degree corners. Carefully fit these around each window covering the joints and about ½″ (12mm) of the window frame and cladding, using 1″ (2.5cm) galvanized panel pins.

At the very top of the roof you have a small flat section covered with lead; it will make a great difference to the finished look of the treehouse to fit a ornamental finial on this. The finial can be whatever you want, from a simple wooden banister finial to an elaborately carved eagle. If you have or know someone who has a lathe and turns wood, an attractive wooden, curved spike like the one that we have used on this treehouse makes a nice finishing detail. A client of mine presented me with a wooden owl that he had meticulously carved, which when placed on the top of his treehouse, looked absolutely superb.

Whatever you choose, make sure it has several coats of stain and is fixed carefully to the top of the roof with a dowel inserted into the base and into the finial, before being sealed into place with an outdoor sealant.

Your attention should now turn to the neoprene collars that we have used to surround the trunk and boughs of the tree as they protrude through the treehouse, allowing the tree to move without harm and preventing water from entering the treehouse. However, depending upon the species, the tree trunk is unlikely to be totally smooth and may well have a heavily ridged bark creating gaps and grooves

The finial in place.

The neoprene collars sitting below the finished cedar shingles. These will need close checking after the first downpour.

Staining the rail.

through which water can come in. These gaps need to be well sealed with a plumber's black gutter sealant. This material never really sets hard and retains a degree of flexibility ideal for this purpose. Work your way around every place where the tree interacts with the treehouse and carefully seal completely around each area until you are confident that all are water tight.

Note: **The only real test of how watertight your treehouse is will come after a long downpour, and it may well be that some parts need re-sealing after you have found a leak or two. Make sure you wait until the area is completely dry before re-sealing.**

Before starting to stain the wood, I always like to paint all pieces of exposed metal work. It is really worth the time and effort doing this as it is surprising how a small piece of bright metal stands out, especially if the sun catches it.

First, use the grinder to remove all sharp edges and exposed bolts that might be dangerous. Use specialist metal work paint in either bark brown or

black—not only will the paint disguise the silver color of the galvanizing, but will also add to the protection of the exposed parts of metal still visible. Work around the entire treehouse carefully painting all brackets and even the heads of all the lag screws. This is a rather tedious process, but well worth it.

The treehouse is constructed almost entirely out of pressure treated wood, so it can only be coated with a stain solution. However, the pressure treatment can only force the preservative so far into the wood, so that any cut pieces of end grain could well be susceptible to damp and rot. I always recommend that the staining is carried out as part of an additional preservative treatment.

Select a good quality, colored preservative for the walls, deck and balustrade, and underside foundations. I would always suggest that you use at least two different colors; in this case we are using three—dark oak, light oak, and a dark green. Nothing in nature is just one color and a treehouse, especially a medium sized structure such as this one, is too large to be one large mass of the same color. However, I understand that colors are very personal and you should decide on what suits you and the surroundings. I would advise that the foundations underneath are stained darker than the rest of the treehouse.

Staining the treehouse foundations dark brown.

Note: **Try to buy a small quantity of each color and test each on a piece of off cut wood of the same sort as you will be staining, to make sure it is right before you start.**

You will need to apply two coats and should start with the walls of the treehouse at the top and work down in sections with a large thick brush, taking extra care and using a smaller brush around the already stained windows and doors.

Note: **The cedar shingles on the roof do not need coating. Cedar contains natural oils and should not be treated.**

Next, coat the decking, staircase, and railings making sure that these are totally dry before applying the second coat.

Finally, the whole of the underneath and foundations of the treehouse should be stained—in this case with a very dark oak color. This is the really messy job where however careful you are, you are likely to get covered in stain. I have found a disposable boiler suit and an old hat to be invaluable for this task.

Once the entire treehouse has had its two coats, it is visually almost complete and ready to take whatever the weather can throw at it.

Variations

Apart from safety, there are remarkably few rules when it comes to building your treehouse. You are free to express yourself and choose from a multitude of materials available. As long as the material you choose is suitable for the outdoors and has the structural characteristics you require, there is nothing stopping you. Below are a few examples of how the overall look of the treehouse can be changed by using different materials in different ways.

A higher treehouse over a lower tree deck showing rope detail and cladding in rough-edged wood.

The shaped detail at the end of an overhanging platform joist—a simple curve from the bottom of a stain can, cut out with a jigsaw.

Staining in blue and red. Not all treehouses have to be green and brown.

Curled thick rope at the end of a stair handrail.

Simple scalloped detail adds a finishing touch to eaves.

Double reversed curves to the ends of these protruding joists.

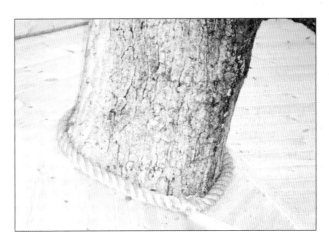

Thick rope detail to the tree trunk as it exits the lined treehouse via the roof.

A small fretwork detail from a cedar off cut helps give an oriental feel to this treehouse.

Rope and cloth detail to the joint of footrail and a bamboo upright. An uplighter is set into the end of the bamboo support.

Accessories

One of the best things about a treehouse is that you can always add and adapt as time moves on and your requirements change. What starts out as your children's playroom could develop into their homework den and teenage hangout, then become your hobby shop or office, be enjoyed as a place of tranquil relaxation, and end up again as a playground for your grandchildren.

A duck pulley with a basket set at the side of a pond, where one client keeps ornamental ducks.

A shaped extended joist with a rope hole through the top half of the joist. This will easily support a button swing or climbing rope.

When it comes to accessories, there is no limit to what you can fit in, on, around, or under your new treehouse and these can easily be added to or changed as you require.

Why not add bookshelves, a bookcase, a wine rack, or a fully fitted kitchen? A rope cargo net makes a great attraction for children of all ages, as does a climbing rope, and a hammock slung underneath the treehouse is a superb place to relax in the shade.

Safety

In most cases it is not the making or fitting of accessories that will cause any safety issues but the usage of these once the treehouse is completed. Especially with children's play equipment it is very important to test each piece before allowing children to use it. Whether children should be allowed to use the treehouse without supervision is obviously a personal decision. Personally over a certain age I think children should

The zip slide in use.

EQUIPMENT

Essential

power drill

jigsaw

handsaw

hand tools

tape measure

spirit level

Useful

battery drill

electric sander

MATERIALS

1″ diameter pressure treated doweling (16′ in length)

2″ x 10″ pressure treated timber

off cuts

wicker basket

½″ diameter rope

zip slide equipment

small pulley

be able to enjoy adventurous play by themselves, but do think they should be supervised initially until they are used to the equipment and well briefed as to how to use each piece.

Note: A zip or cable slide is potentially a dangerous piece of equipment and a great deal of thought should be given before fitting one—there is no doubt it will prove to be a magnet to children of all ages. My best advice is to make sure the zip slide you install has a seat and not just handles and make sure the seat can be detached and stored at times when younger children are using the treehouse.

A close-up of a traditional rope swing.

A close up of a button swing.

SAFETY CHECK

• **Make sure all play equipment is thoroughly checked before use.**

• **Make sure children are always supervised or well briefed.**

• **Only fit a zip slide that is suitable for the task—one that has been tested and accredited, and with a seat.**

• **Take care when hanging the pulley for the basket above the veranda. Make sure you are tied on firmly.**

Key objectives

- Make a traditional swing to suspend under the treehouse.
- Suspend a basket and pulley to pull up provisions to the treehouse veranda.
- Fit the zip (cable) slide.
- Make and fix a rope ladder up and on to the main front veranda.
- Make a simple button swing.

The swing hung in place.

The completed swing seat.

To make a traditional swing, cut a piece of 2″ x 10″ (5 x 25cm) wood to 30″ (76cm).

By hand, draw a slightly curving line around the outline of the rectangle to give a softer and more natural form and follow this line with your jigsaw. With great care, use a sharp knife to carve away the sharp edge completely around both sides of the roughed out piece of wood.

You can be quite artistic as you carve; the softer and more freeform the end shape the better. Next, drill two ¾″ (19mm) holes at each end 7″ (17cm) apart and 1½″ (38mm) from the end. The entire swing seat now has to be well sanded—top, bottom, and sides—to create a smooth and interesting shaped seat. An electric sander will allow you to complete the task quicker and even create some shape into the flat surface of the wood. Three or four coats of an external varnish will make this a very special swing indeed.

Decide where you wish to hang your swing under the treehouse; it will need to be directly under and in line with one of the main foundation wood pieces. Mark two points 27″ (68cm) apart on the chosen beam, 6″ (15cm) from the bottom and drill a ½″ (12mm) hole directly through the beam at these points. Measure the height of the holes through the beam to the floor and cut two pieces of rope at twice that length. Thread each of the pieces of rope through the holes in the beam until they are exactly halfway through, then take each end and thread through the seat you have just prepared.

Lift the seat off the ground about 20″ (50cm) by sliding it up the ropes and loosely tie the ropes underneath the swing, making sure the seat is exactly level, and then tie the ropes off permanently.

A wicker basket suspended over the side of the treehouse veranda is not only a good talking point but is also practical for pulling up provisions or toys from the ground below. A small lightweight pulley suitable for a washing line, for example, will normally be available from a hardware store. This should be attached to a higher branch above the treehouse veranda and very slightly further out past the railings. Through this pulley, a suitable rope should be threaded and cut to length, ensuring that the rope can touch the ground while still leaving plenty at the veranda end to pull up. A hook attached to the veranda rail will mean that the rope will never totally disappear and the other end should be tied tightly around the basket handle. Then haul away!

A zip slide or cable slide is likely to be the greatest attraction of any treehouse from children of about six or seven years of age up to "big kids" of 40 plus. The feeling of dropping off the edge of a platform and whizzing down a line never loses its attraction. However, a zip side needs to be installed with great care and the component parts must be of top quality—designed to do the task safely, time after time, even after being left outside for months or years.

I strongly advise never to install a zip slide with a handle bar rather than a seat. Any person, however

The basket and pulley in place.

young or old, can lose their grip, especially when excited or wet. A seat, however, gives easier support and in my opinion is much safer.

My company has searched the world for the best zip slide component parts and we found them in Denmark. The system we use is suspended on ⅜″ (10mm) 19 strand stainless-steel cable, capable of holding up to 6 tons! Onto this we fix the trolley, which again is stainless steel— it is fully enclosed so it would be impossible to trap your fingers and has an automatic breaking system. The seat is molded plastic and this molding continues up the chain to the point where it joins the trolley, eliminating any possibility of pinching. The break system consists of a rubber block with a 10′ (3m) or 18′ (5.4m) spring that tenses as it is compressed and causes the trolley to slowly and gently come to a rest. The cable is suspended between two

The route that the completed zip slide will take to the distant tree through the wooded area around the treehouse.

Adjustable ratchet mechanism for the zip slide.

steel devises that can, with a system of pulleys and ratchets, easily adjust the tension on the cable and therefore the rate of descent.

The tension block is bolted to a suitable tree trunk of bough 8'–10' (2.4–3m) above the platform height. The receiving block is bolted to a suitable tree, slightly lower than the height of the first block between 50' and 300' (15 and 91m) apart from each other. The zip slide fitted from the treehouse we are following is 100' (30cm) from one tree to the other.

The trolley and break devise is threaded along the cable which is then attached by the clamps provided at both ends. Using the tensioner, the cable is wound up to a point where the cable still hangs in a loop but is about 6'–8' (2–2.4m) above the ground at its lowest point.

At this point, the seat can be hung from the trolley on a screw fixed carabineer, which will allow the seat to be removed easily and stored out of the way if required.

After testing all the joints and making sure that all bolts have been tightened, it is time to test the slide. Unfortunately it is only by testing it that you can adjust the zip slide so that it runs at the best speed and stops gently at the end, so expect a few bumpy rides.

Once you have adjusted the tension in the cable to give the best ride, it is time to let other people try the system. After adjusting again to get the best ride for all weights, the tensioner can be locked into position. The zip slide is now ready to use—always with care, and with younger children it is advisable to use with supervision.

The rope ladder requires another ten pieces of 1" (2.5cm) dowel cut to 1' 9" (53cm). Two inches in from each end of the pieces of dowel, mark a line right around the dowel. With a sharp knife, make a shallow grooved ring following your line completely around each end of each dowel. Cut your rope into two pieces and lay out on a level surface 1′ 6″ (45cm) apart from each other. Next to each piece of rope, make a mark at each 10″ (25cm) interval.

At the point of each mark, carefully split the rope as evenly as possible and slide in the dowel to the point of the groove. Above and below each dowel, tightly bind the rope that will grip the dowel and the groove will stop it slipping sideways. Once all the treads are in place, the top of the rope ladder can be fixed centrally below the safety rails.

I prefer to bind the bottom two ropes together and form a loop, which can be hooked over a stake driven into the ground. This makes climbing the rope ladder much easier, especially if the children are not used to it, but still allows the rope ladder to be pulled up on to the deck if required.

Making a button swing is simply a variation of the traditional swing described above. Instead of cutting out a rectangle, draw a circle 10″ (25cm) in diameter on an off cut of 2″ x 10″ (5 x 25cm). Cut around this shape with a jigsaw but do not follow the line exactly. Give the seat some shape and form by varying the cut over and under the line drawn. Once you have your free-formed circular seat cut out, use a sharp knife to bevel the edge, taking away the sharpness and creating even more shape. Drill a ½″ (12.7mm) hole completely through the center point of the seat and sand the block smooth on both sides and around the edges, softening the appearance. Give the finished seat three coats of exterior varnish and leave to dry.

This time the swing will be suspended from just one rope, so find the best spot under the treehouse

A rope ladder hanging in place against the treehouse veranda.

and drill a ½″ (12.7mm) hole through one of the foundation wood pieces 6″ (15cm) from the bottom edge. Thread a ½″ (12.7mm) rope through this hole and tie a large double knot on one side of the joist. The other end gets threaded through the swing seat and tied loosely underneath, about 2′ (60cm) from the ground. Check that this height is suitable for the children who will use the swing and then permanently tie. Cut off the loose trailing rope.

Interiors

A completed interior of a treehouse.

The exterior of your treehouse is now complete and it is sealed and watertight. Now is the time to start on the interior finishings. The way that you furnish and decorate your treehouse will of course depend very much on the purpose that you are going to use it for. A tree office, for example, is likely to have a desk, either fitted or freestanding, storage in cupboards, drawers and shelves, and space for computers, printers, phones and all the normal modern office requirements. It may have a small area for tea or coffee making but is unlikely to have much casual furniture, whereas a teenage den will probably have tables and soft chairs as well as a TV and almost certainly a sound system!

The treehouse we have followed throughout this book is intended to be used as a family space, with no single particular function; somewhere the children can play by themselves and with friends and

EQUIPMENT
Essential

jigsaw

handsaw

tape measure

spirit level

MATERIALS

1 sheet—4′ x 8′ best quality plywood
(¾″ in thickness)

1 sheet—4′ x 8′ cheap plywood
(¼″ in thickness)

hinges to suit

table between the boughs, which can be removed when required, allowing the upturned hand shape to be converted with soft cushions into a unique area to lounge around.

as they get older have parties and do homework, and also somewhere that the owners can escape and read a paper or have quiet evening drinks. Because of this multi-function usage we didn't want to fill the treehouse with fitted furniture or storage, just a simple

With the correct lighting and music, this treehouse can be given many moods, from the place for a cool party to a location for a sophisticated dinner. A nice sunny day can transform your treehouse to a den for young children, full of noise and laughter and can just as easily transform into a place for simple tranquil contemplation.

I cannot think of a better place to read a book or make my way through the Sunday papers with a cup of coffee.

The finished table in the space previously measured by the author (see page 33).

Children's treehouse interior with bright colors and a toy snake up in the loft sleeping area.

Presuming that you have fitted your treehouse with insulation and are having an electric heater or maybe an oilfilled radiator, the treehouse can be used all year round. The only limit to what you do with your treehouse is your imagination and the best place to make the most of your imagination is in a tree, high up above the ground. To give you more ideas of how the inside of your treehouse may be finished, this section shows examples of interior treatments and how they were created.

Safety

Working inside the treehouse should be relatively safe and our only concern will be the use of power tools.

SAFETY CHECK

• **Take care when using power tools and make sure you use protective equipment as required.**

Key objectives

• Rub down and seal the interior walls and floor
• Construct a table to fit in and around the tree trunks

As previously mentioned I am very keen on keeping the inside of treehouses light and bright, so I tend not to advise staining the interior. Instead I prefer giving all the interior wood—walls, framework and ceiling—a very good rub down with sandpaper.

I start with a medium grade and finish with a fine grade and then two coats of exterior furniture oil. The oil should be applied with a cloth and generously rubbed into the wood. The first coat will soak in quite easily and the second will leave a nice sheen without lying on the surface.

The furniture oil will give a long lasting seal to the walls and ceiling but is not tough enough for the floor. After sanding the floor with medium sandpaper you should give it three or four coats of clear matt floor varnish. The first coat should be thinned with paint thinner by about 25%, though the next coats can be straight from the can. Always give plenty of drying time between each coat and enough ventilation to the room when applying.

The table is designed to be easily removed and stored, and will fit between the branches in the center, making an interesting and useful feature that can be folded in two and stored if not required.

The first task is to create a template for the finished table on the cheaper ¼" (64mm) plywood. Making a template allows you to make an occasional mistake without spoiling an expensive sheet of ¾" (1.9cm) ply and, equally important, is much easier to handle. This is an awkward and tricky procedure.

Place the piece of plywood on the floor near the branches and slowly rotate it, looking to see in what position it will fit and give most room when used as a table. Remember that you will cut a freeform

With no need to re-create the sophisticated style of the family home, this simple interior has a window bench seat carved roughly from 2″ x 8″ (5 x 20cm) lumber and then sanded and wiped with furniture oil until smooth, complementing the table around the tree trunk in the foreground.

edge around the table so don't worry at this stage about the square protruding corners. Once you have it placed in the best position, start to draw, in a rough freehand, the shape that will be cut out, allowing the table to slip downwards and fit into position between the boughs.

Note: You will gradually be cutting away at the plywood until you achieve exactly the right shape to fit the tree. It is better to cut too little than too much, so take your time and make smaller cuts each time rather than rushing the job.

Making sure that you do not cut too much at this stage, cut around your line with a jigsaw. Lift the

plywood, place it between the branches and level off, using a spirit level in all directions. The plywood will probably be sitting too high and only fitting the tree in a few places. Leaving the ply in place, draw another line where you will make your next cut which will start to lower the template into its final position.

Note: If accidentally you cut too much in one place, make a mark on the template indicating this and by how much it should be extended in this area.

Eventually you will have the template sitting exactly in place with any gaps marked. You can now draw around the template onto the ¾″ (1.9cm) plywood taking into account any adjustments that you need to make. With someone to help you lift the thick plywood into place, and presuming it fits exactly, you can draw around the outer edge where you want the table to finish. Next draw a straight line across the center of the table at the best place for the table to fold.

Taking the table back off again, cut around the outer edge line with the jigsaw and make the straight cut across the center with the handsaw. Give all of the table edges a good sanding with medium sandpaper, followed by a fine sandpaper. Wipe the surface and edges of the table with a cloth and paint thinner and leave to dry. The table then should be stained, again with a soft cloth, before being coated with two coats of varnish (the same varnish as used on the floor will be fine.)

Put the two top faces of the table together and line up the straight center edge cut. Carefully notch out a recess in the wood to insert a pair of butt hinges and fix into position into the edge of the plywood with 1½″ (38mm) screws.

A simple table built from off cuts of floorboards makes a great feature around this large oak tree trunk

The table should be quite easy to manage now and should be lifted into place and folded open ready to use. The treehouse interior shown below is not lined internally, as it was intended for summer use only as opposed to a year-round space.

The owners of this treehouse were very specific about one particular point. They wanted a rustic retreat where they could entertain and insisted that the ceiling was left open so that the underside of the cedar shingles were on view. This meant that unlike the treehouse that we have been following, where the roof was boarded with plywood prior to shingling, this roof was strapped with ½" x 1" (1.27 x 2.5cm) battens onto which the shingles were nailed. The result is an interesting roof that adds character to the room, especially with a skylight situated immediately over the kitchen area. A small sink with hot and cold running water, a fridge, microwave and small oven allow guests to be served hot and cold food as they sit between the solid oak table which is suspended

This dining room in the sky manages to preserve the simple rustic feel requested by the owners.

The simple style chosen for this interior space is achieved by using loose cushions, a rug, and low stools. It's the perfect place to chill and chat with friends during the school holidays.

between five large boughs of this mature willow tree. You will notice the use of careful lighting, wooden ornaments and ironwork furniture, which adds to the natural charm of the room.

One advantage of not lining the interior of your treehouse is that you can use the exposed framing joists as shelves. The disadvantage is that in some treehouses an unlined roof can be a lot darker than one which has been clad in softwood.

To accommodate a large amount of toys that were to be brought up into the treehouse when completed, a toybox in the treehouse below was built using the same materials as the walls. 2″ x 3″ (5 x 7.5cm) lumber was cut to length and the frame was screwed together incorporating the floor and two

Above: Fold-down bunk beds on chains increase interior space. They can be folded away when not in use.

Below: The rocking horse that could not fit into the large toy box stands guard in this attractive and unique children's playroom.

walls as sides. This frame was clad in the same way as the walls on the front and remaining end. The lid was made separately to fit exactly into place and then hinged at the rear against the original wall-framing joist. When complete, the box was stencilled before being given two coats of a hardwearing varnish.

One of the nicest things about being up in a tree on a bright sunny day is the way in which the branches and leaves break up the light, giving a dappled effect. The inclusion of stained glass into windows can create patches of colored light on the internal walls and floor. In that case, the need for painting the walls in bright colors is diminished.

Below: Sometimes the interior space needs no work at all; like this rustic treehouse where the interior is totally dominated by oak tree trunks and branches.

Above: The same bunk beds, as left, folded and out of the way.

Maintenance

In terms of maintenance, a treehouse has one huge advantage over a wooden ground-based structure—it is suspended high above the earth. The main problem that occurs in any wooden building is that its base often lies in water and, even in reasonably dry conditions, it tends to draw up moisture from below. This is why a wooden building still needs a stone or brick foundation to lift it off the ground and a damp proof course to stop the dry wood sucking up water through the foundations.

A treehouse has none of these requirements. Any rain water will tend to fall off down to the ground below and while the tree itself draws up vast amounts of water to feed its new twigs and leaves, this will not cause the treehouse any harm. By using pressure treated wood with natural oils, such as cedar, the treehouse is likely not to suffer from the ravages of rot and decay to the same extent.

However, it still makes sense to protect your investment and the hard work you put into the treehouse. All exposed wood, walls, decking, railings, stairs, ladders, windows, doors, and foundations should be recoated with a preservative every 2 years.

You have the choice of using a colored preservative to freshen up the look of the treehouse or you can use a clear preservative that will treat and protect the wood, without spoiling the natural aging process that starts to blend the treehouse into the tree.

Every year you need to carry out a thorough check of the following items:

Check all nuts, bolts, and coach screws, making sure that none show indications of weakness and are all tightened if any looseness is felt.

Check all metalwork to ensure that brackets haven't moved and look at the foundation wood pieces for signs of wear and tear. Once you are completely happy that the structure of the treehouse is sound, you can move on to the areas where the treehouse meets the tree. In building the treehouse, we should not have harmed the tree in any way and it should be continuing to grow as normal. Luckily the vast majority of tree growth happens at the very end of the branches and the growth that occurs in the area where you will have constructed your treehouse will be very limited. However, it is important that every place where a branch runs through a platform, wall, or roof is checked, first to ensure that the tree is not rubbing against the solid structure as it moves in the wind and second, to make sure that the hole cut around the branch or trunk is not starting to strangle the tree. If either of these important matters is discovered, you will need to extend the size of the hole by using a jigsaw and then reseal as you did originally. At the same time that you are checking for possible areas of current or future tree damage, you should also check for leaks and reseal as required.

Now that you have checked the structural stability of the treehouse, the tree's health, and the continued weather tightness of the treehouse, you can then do the normal and less-pressing maintenance, such as adjusting the window hinges and latches, the door locks, and giving the treehouse a quick spring cleaning.

Regular maintenance will not only keep your treehouse safe and ensure that it lasts as long as possible, but it will also guarantee it looks its best all the time. After spending so much time in the construction, it makes sense to keep it looking its best.

Index

Imperial/metric conversion chart

⅛ inch = 3mm	14 inches = 35cm
¼ inch = 5mm	15 inches = 38cm
½ inch = 1cm	16 inches = 40cm
¾ inch = 2cm	18 inches/1½ feet
1 inch = 2.5cm	= 45cm
1½ inch = 4cm	20 inches = 50cm
2 inches = 5cm	21 inches = 52cm
2½ inches = 6cm	24 inches/2 feet
3 inches = 7.5cm	= 60cm
4 inches = 10cm	25 inches = 62cm
4½ inches = 12cm	26 inches = 65cm
5 inches = 13cm	27 inches = 68cm
5½ inches = 14cm	2½ feet = 75cm
6 inches = 15cm	36 inches /3 feet
6¼ inches = 16cm	= 90cm
6½ inches = 17cm	1 yard = 1m
7 inches = 18cm	4 feet = 1.2m
8 inches = 20cm	1½ yards = 1.5m
8½ inches = 21cm	7 feet = 2.1m
9 inches = 23cm	90 inches /7½ feet
10 inches = 25cm	= 2.3m
10½ inches = 27cm	115 inches /9½ feet
11 inches = 28cm	= 2.9m
12 inches/1 foot	150 inches /12½ feet
= 30cm	= 3.8m
13 inches = 33cm	30 feet/10 yds = 10m

Acknowledgments

Dedication

To all the people connected with the TreeHouse Company and its continued success.

Especially the treehouse builders who were involved in the construction of this particular treehouse: Willie McCubbin, Jim Wales, Brian Keown, Peter Tudhope, Derek Sanderson, and Alex Shirley-Smith.

Many thanks to my client Mr. and Mrs. David Hearson and their children who allowed their treehouse to be featured in this book. I hope they enjoy using it for many years to come.

As always, my wife Moira for her patience and enthusiasm for what I do.

John Harris

www.treehouse-company.com

Picture Acknowledgments

All images © Chrysalis Image Library / Simon Clay 2004 apart from the following exceptions.

T = Top B = Bottom R = Right L = Left

© Authors Collection p5 (figs: 2, 4, 5, 6, 7, 8, 9, 10), p6, p7, p8, p9, p10, p11, p12, p13, p14, p15, p28TR, p31, p32, p34, p35, p36, p37, p38, p39TL, p39TR, p40, p44, p47, p60, p61, p74, p75, p86, p87, p96, p97, p98, p104, p105, p110BL, p111, p112, p113, p114, p116, p117, p124, p125, p126, p127BL, p127BR, p134, p135, p136, p137, p138, p139.